Christianity and world religions

CHRISTIANITY AND WORLD RELIGIONS
The challenge of Pluralism

SIR NORMAN ANDERSON
O.B.E., Q.C., LL.D., F.B.A.

*formerly Professor of Oriental Laws,
and Director of the Institute of Advanced Legal Studies,
in the University of London*

INTER–VARSITY PRESS
LEICESTER, ENGLAND
DOWNERS GROVE, ILLINOIS, U.S.A.

INTER-VARSITY PRESS
38 De Montfort Street, Leicester LE1 7GP, England
Box 1400, Downers Grove, Illinois 60515, U.S.A.

*Inter-Varsity Press, England, is the publishing division of the Universities and Colleges
Christian Fellowship (formerly the Inter-Varsity Fellowship), a student movement linking
Christian Unions in universities and colleges throughout the United Kingdom and the
Republic of Ireland, and a member movement of the International Fellowship of Evangelical
Students. For information about local and national activities, write to
UCCF, 38 De Montfort Street, Leicester LE1 7GP.* 🏛️

*InterVarsity Press, U.S.A., is the book-publishing division of Inter-Varsity Christian
Fellowship, a student movement active on campus at hundreds of universities, colleges
and schools of nursing. For information about local and regional activities, write IVCF,
233 Langdon St., Madison, WI 53703.*

*Typeset in 11/12 pt Palatino in Great Britain by Nuprint Services Ltd, Harpenden, Herts.
Printed in the United States of America*

British Library Cataloguing in Publication Data
Anderson, Norman
    Christianity and world religions.–2nd ed.
    1. Religions
    I. Title   II. Anderson, Norman.
    Christianity and comparative religion
    291   BL80.2

    ISBN 0-85111-323-0

Library of Congress Cataloging in Publication Data
Anderson, J. N. D. (James Norman Dalrymple), Sir, 1908-
    Christianity and world religions.

    Rev. ed. of: Christianity and comparative religion. 1971, c1970.
    Bibliography: p.
    Includes indexes.
    1. Christianity and other religions.   I. Anderson,
J. N. D. (James Norman Dalrymple), Sir, 1908-
Christianity and comparative religion.   II. Title.
BR127.A75   1984   261.2   84-115291
ISBN 0-87784-981-1 (U.S.)

18	17	16	15	14	13	12	11	10	9	8	7	6
98	97	96	95	94	93	92						

Contents

Foreword

Some fourteen years ago I wrote a book entitled *Christianity and Comparative Religion*. This was based on the Church of Ireland's series of theological lectures which I had been asked to give for 1970 in the Queen's University of Belfast. The book was published the same year by the Tyndale Press in England and the Inter-Varsity Press in the United States, and has been reprinted several times on both sides of the Atlantic. Now, however, it is virtually out of print, and I have been asked to bring it up to date. Hence the present volume.

I had at first intended to entitle this book *Christianity and Comparative Religion: the Challenge of Pluralism* in order to indicate that this new book has retained much of the basic structure, and a considerable amount of the detailed substance, of its predecessor, but in a revised and substantially expanded form – partly in the light of much that has been written on the subject in recent years, and partly in response to the major change there has been from an emphasis on what may be termed old-fashioned Syncretism to a fully-fledged Pluralism. But it also seemed desirable to change the first part of the title from *Christianity and Comparative Religion* to *Christianity and World Religions* – partly because the term 'comparative' in this context has always, strictly speaking, been a misnomer (as I pointed out from the beginning), but chiefly because people are far more concerned with the vital question of world religions than with a discipline of studying them in any particular way. But, be that as it may, the continuing debate about the world's great religions and their relation to the Christian faith certainly underlines the importance of a subject that continues to provoke such a diversity of opinion between experts and a widening interest among the public at large.

There has in fact been a positive spate of publications on this topic during the intervening years, only a few of which can here be mentioned in passing. Authors who had written quite extensively in the past on certain aspects of this subject have produced further volumes, and there has been an interesting tendency for some of them to turn from their particular expertise to a more comprehensive view. Kenneth Cragg, for example, after publishing some three more books since 1970 on various aspects of Islam, has now written one on *The Christian and Other Religion* (Oxford, 1977). Wilfred Cantwell Smith, again, has recently turned from detailed studies of Islam to such subjects as *Belief and History* (Charlottesville, 1977), *Faith and Belief* (Princeton, 1979) and *Towards a World Theology* (London, 1981) – although it is true that he had started to paint on a world-wide canvas several years before. Somewhat similarly, John V. Taylor has widened his primary concentration on African religion first to his book *The Go-Between God: the Holy Spirit and the Christian Mission* (London, 1972) and then to a lecture on 'The Theological Basis of Interfaith Dialogue' (delivered as the first Lambeth Interfaith Lecture in 1977).

Many other writers have launched out into similar waters during the last few years. Geoffrey Parrinder, for example, has followed his *Avatar and Incarnation* (London, 1970) with a second edition of his *Worship in the World's Religions* (London, 1974) and with *Upanishads, Gītā and the Bible* (London, 1975). Ninian Smart has been equally active, with *The Religious Experience of Mankind* (New York, 1971), *The Concept of Worship* (London, 1972) and *The Phenomenon of Religion* (London, 1973). Among other recent books on this general subject, written from widely different standpoints, may be mentioned Charles Davis's *Christ and the World Religions* (London, 1970), Peter Beyerhaus's *Missions: which way? Humanization or redemption* (E.T., Grand Rapids, 1971), Raimundo Panikkar's *The Trinity and the Religious*

Experience of Man (New York and London, 1973) and *The Intra-Religious Dialogue* (New York, 1978), R. J. Zwi Werblowsky's *Beyond Tradition and Modernity* (London, 1976), James W. Sire's *The Universe Next Door* (Illinois, 1976). Jens Christensen's *The Practical Approach to Muslims* (Marseilles, 1977), Lesslie Newbigin's *The Open Secret* (Grand Rapids, 1978) and J. A. T. Robinson's *Truth is Two-Eyed* (London, 1979). I have myself published *God's Law and God's Love: an Essay in Comparative Religion* (London, 1980) and an introductory essay on 'Christianity and the World's Religions' in the first volume of *The Expositor's Bible Commentary* (ed. Frank Gaebelein, Grand Rapids, 1979).

Quite a lot of work in this field has also been done by those whose primary interest has been centred on religious education. In this context the names of writers such as J. R. Hinnells, F. H. Hilliard, W. Owen Cole, D. W. Grundy and Edward Hulmes (and especially his work as Director of the Farmington Institute) come especially to mind.

The participants in this 'continuing debate' come from a wide variety of backgrounds and, almost inevitably, express sharply divergent views. There can be little doubt, however, that some of the most articulate and controversial contributions have come from John Hick, of Birmingham and the Claremont Graduate School of Religion, California, whose own theological approach has changed radically during the last few years. He himself gives expression to this change, in part, when he explains why a book published in 1968 under the title *Christianity at the Centre* was republished in 1977, in a revised and enlarged edition, as *The Centre of Christianity*. He has spelt out his views in considerably more detail, however, in *God and the Universe of Faiths* (London, 1973) and *God Has Many Names* (London, 1980). Both these last two volumes, moreover, bring together in a convenient form a number of his recent essays and lectures (some of them revised and some virtually verbatim) – including the chapter on 'Jesus and the World Religions' which was his own contribution to the symposium he edited under the title of *The Myth of God Incarnate* (London, 1977). So it will, I think, make for clarity if I concentrate primarily on these recent publications (all of which are, I think, readily available) in the comments I propose to make in this present volume on some of the major points at issue in the continuing debate.

Norman Anderson

1

Introduction

Comparative religion

What used to be called 'comparative religion' is a subject which arouses a lively and widespread concern today. Strictly speaking, the very term is, of course, a misnomer – which is, no doubt, one reason why alternative terms are increasingly being coined and used; for it is not 'religion' itself which is 'comparative' but the way in which it is studied and approached. But to speak of 'the comparative study of religion', or 'the comparative study of law', seems unnecessarily pedantic, although it should be stated emphatically that this is what comparative religion or comparative law really means. As such, comparative religion is simply one aspect of the study of religion.

In a book published some years ago under the title of *Comparative Religion in Education* (edited by J. R. Hinnells), reference was made to 'the remarkable popularity of "world religions" as a subject for academic and semi-academic study in Western educational institutions. Universities, colleges of education, seminaries and theological colleges, secondary schools and part-time classes are all, in their various ways, attempting to meet what is in process of becoming a widespread popular desire for insights into the beliefs and practices of religions other than Christianity.' And Eric J. Sharpe suggested that the reasons for this 'upsurge of enthusiasm for a subject which until a few years ago remained the province of a very few specialists' can be found in improved communications with other lands, insistent questioning of the role of the West *vis-à-vis* non-Western peoples, increased availability of information on the popular level, the presence in our midst of ever larger numbers of adherents of non-Western religious traditions, and also a growing feeling of disillusionment with organized Christianity and with the intellectual foundations of Western society, all of which have combined to 'turn increasing numbers of people – and not least young people – towards a new quest for "light from the East"' (Hinnells, p.1).[1] Other reasons might, of course, also be given, such as dissatisfaction with an affluent and technologically sophisticated society, a revolt from the contemporary 'rat race', the barrenness of intellectual humanism, and a desire to make religious education both more interesting and more obviously relevant to modern life.

The subject is formidable in the extreme, for it has expanded so rapidly that it is often broken down today into the history of religion, the phenomenology of religion, the psychology of religion, the sociology of religion and the philosophy of religion (*cf*. Hinnells, p.9) – although it must be emphasized that the phenomenological and historical study of religion are not necessarily comparative. Naturally enough, therefore, it has repeatedly been emphasized that no one scholar can ever hope to cover the whole field. This is, indeed, obvious when one realizes that, in spite of all the classical texts which have been translated into Western languages and all that has been written on the subject, it is exceedingly difficult – if not impossible – really to enter into the meaning and ethos of another religion without an intimate acquaintance with those who put that religion into practice in their daily lives and, ideally, a competent knowledge of the language or languages, or at least the culture and circumstances, in which its basic literature was written. This means that we are left with only three alternatives: the first-hand assessment of a limited field by an

---

[1] Reference to other books and sources is given in abbreviated form, using the author's name only, or author and title where there are two or more works by the same author quoted in this present volume. Full bibliographical details are given in the Bibliography (see pp.00ff.).

individual scholar; a broad survey of a wide field based largely on second-hand materials; or a collaborative study by a number of different scholars.

But students of world religions do not differ among themselves only in their linguistic and scholarly equipment, but also in their religious convictions. Ideally, from one point of view, they should have no preconceived ideas at all and should approach the subject in an attitude of complete detachment. But while this might facilitate a ruthless objectivity, it would almost certainly hinder any deep understanding; for it seems probable that the secrets of religion are almost as inaccessible to one who is himself devoid of any religious conviction as are those of music to one who is tone deaf. 'No one', as Wilfred Cantwell Smith has remarked, 'has understood the diverse faiths of mankind if his so-called explanation of them makes fundamental nonsense of each one' (*The Faith of Other Men*, p. 13). In any case, a complete freedom from preconceived ideas is a practical impossibility; and in my experience the unbeliever is just as much conditioned by his unbelief as the believer is by his faith.

Statistics about religious affiliation are seldom reliable. This is not only, or even primarily, because census figures are themselves often both unreliable and hard to come by, but because no census figures can throw much light on the variety of beliefs and practices which prevail in many countries or the increasing number of those who have largely rejected their ancestral faiths. Within several of the great world religions, moreover, there is a wide variety of sects and schools of thought. At a rough estimate, however, there must be more than 1,000 million of those who belong to what is often termed the 'Judaeo-Christian tradition', and a somewhat larger number made up, in roughly equal proportions, of Muslims and Hindus. There are also several hundred million Buddhists, some of whom combine Confucian, Taoist, Shintōist or other teachings with their Buddhism; and, by a rather different method of calculation, there are hundreds of millions of Chinese who might be classified as Communists, Confucianists, Taoists or Buddhists, and frequently combine elements from two or more of these sources. There must be some fifty million Japanese

13

adherents of Shintōism[2]; about eight million Sikhs; some two million Zoroastrians and two million Jains; perhaps one million Bahā'īs; and a very large but indeterminate number of persons who still follow some pre-literary or tribal religion.[3]

There are, of course, Christians who would object to including Christianity in any study of comparative religion – usually on the ground that what they mean by Christianity is not a system or institutionalized religion as such, but the revelation of God in Jesus and the invitation of the gospel, and that these are absolutely *sui generis*. Thus W. A. Visser 't Hooft remarks that so often Christians themselves

> give the impression that they consider Christianity as a species of the genus religion, as a sub-division of the general human preoccupation with the divine... Since the eighteenth century, and especially since Schleiermacher, this reduction of Christianity to a province of the wide empire of religion has become so widely accepted that most Christians are shocked and surprised when they are told that this view of Christianity is a modern invention which has no foundation whatever in the Bible. Karl Barth has said, 'Neo-Protestantism is religionism', for it has systematically sought to interpret the Christian faith in categories which were taken from a general philosophy of religion rather than in categories provided by the Christian faith itself (Hooft, pp.94f.).

But is it not undeniable, most people will instinctively retort, that Christianity is a religion? If religion is defined as 'Action or conduct indicating a belief in, reverence for, and desire to please, a divine ruling power; the exercise or practice of rites or observances implying this... A particular system of faith and worship... Recognition on the part of man of some higher unseen power as having control of his destiny, and as being entitled to obedience, reverence, and

---

[2] Although a considerably larger number of Shintōists is sometimes claimed. There is both 'State' (or 'Shrine') Shintō and 'Sect' Shintō, which is basically a nature religion, into which much Buddhist and some Taoist beliefs have been incorporated.

[3] It is also noteworthy that other traditional beliefs and practices colour the daily lives of millions who claim to be Christians, Muslims or adherents of other world religions. *Cf.*, *inter alia*, S. M. Zwemer, *The Influence of Animism on Islam*.

worship; the general mental and moral attitude resulting from this belief . . .' (*Shorter Oxford English Dictionary*), then it is impossible to deny that Christianity qualifies for inclusion. So it is perfectly in order to compare it – as I shall attempt to do in the course of these chapters – with other religions. Clearly, if there is such a phenomenon as a genus 'religion', then Christianity (as a convenient label for a complex of phenomena which reflect a system of belief associated with both worship and conduct) is a species in it, in the same formal sense that Islam and Hinduism are. But these labels all represent abstractions. The Christian must, therefore, continually remind himself that no man is 'saved' by Christianity as a religion, but only by the gospel as such (*i.e.* the saving action of God as recorded and interpreted in the New Testament). This is different *in kind* not only from the non-Christian religious systems, but also, in a very real sense, from Christianity itself, when viewed as a system. Man-in-Christianity lies under the judgment of God in the same way, and for the same reasons, as man-in-paganism.

The fact is that generalizations about religion are almost always misleading. Nothing could be further from the truth than the dictum of John Haynes Holmes that 'Religion has not many voices, but only one', for even the most elementary study of the different religions reveals fundamental contradictions. Most of the world's religions have, it is true, developed an ecclesiastical hierarchy of some sort, certain rituals or forms of worship, and also – though less universally – a pattern of moral and ceremonial behaviour to which the fellowship of the faithful is expected to conform. Comparative studies in these fields by sociologists, anthropologists and other scholars may, of course, be very valuable and instructive. But even the most cursory examination of the theology of these different religions reveals far more contradiction than consensus.

By way of introduction to the studies which will follow, it is essential, I think, to comment, in this introductory chapter, on three phenomena which inevitably face any student on this subject – each of which may be said to blur the lines, or minimize the differences, between the many religions which compete for men's allegiance. First, then, we shall consider Syncretism, which is a term *properly* applied, to quote the *Oxford English Dictionary*, to the 'attempted union or reconciliation of diverse or opposite tenets or practices, especially in philosophy or religion'. Next, we must discuss another approach which is not infrequently referred to as 'syncretistic' in a looser sense of that term, but which is more correctly described as Religious Pluralism or even 'the Universe of Faiths'. In practice, however, it is almost impossible to keep these two concepts wholly distinct, for one and the same writer will at one moment speak in terms which could be described as 'syncretic' in the stricter sense and at the next moment in words which would properly apply to a wide plurality of religions which, whatever their differences and explicit contradictions, are assumed somehow to come to the same thing in the end. Thirdly, we must turn our attention briefly to Mysticism, the concepts and practices of which are to be found in almost all the world's religions.

It is essential to give careful attention to each of these phenomena, because our constant criterion must always be the truth rather than any mere dictates of pragmatism. So we must not gloss over the contradictions between one religion and another, take any such sympathetic a view of the mingling of different religions as one may well take of the fusing of different races, or (regarding atheism as the common enemy) try to defend a united 'religious' front at all costs. Loose thinking will get us nowhere. The world today is characterized not only by rampant atheism but also by an almost feverish curiosity about religion and a wistful, and sometimes frantic, quest for something which transcends mere materialism; and this longing for reality must not be fobbed off with a synthetic and misleading solution.

Syncretism

It is, indeed, this very quest for reality, when seen in the light of the pressing need for men and women of different races, cultures and backgrounds to learn to understand each other and work together for the common good, that provides the major incentive for a syncretistic approach to religious differences, or even for dreams of the eventual emergence of one universal world-religion. But before we succumb to any such temptation we must see clearly what Syncretism means.

'Real syncretism', as A. Oepke asserts, 'is always based on the presupposition that all positive religions are only reflections of a universal original religion and show therefore only gradual differences.' So the syncretic approach may be defined as 'the view which holds that there is no unique revelation in history, that there are many different ways to reach the divine reality, that all formulations of religious truth or experience are by their very nature inadequate expressions of that truth and that it is necessary to harmonise as much as possible all religious ideas and experiences so as to create one universal religion for mankind' (Hooft, p.11).

Nor is Syncretism any new phenomenon. It was found in ancient Israel, where it was vehemently denounced by the prophets. It was characteristic of Hellenism and Gnosticism and was widespread in the Roman Empire, where the Emperor Alexander Severus 'had in his private chapel not only the statues of the deified emperors, but also those of the miracle worker Apollonius of Tyana, of Christ, of Abraham and of Orpheus' (Hooft, p.15). It found one of its most powerful advocates in a Muslim emperor, Akbar the Great, who tried to create a new, universal religion. His vision was to bring the different religions of the Moghul empire into one, 'but in such fashion that they should be both "one" and "all"; with the great advantage of not losing what is good in one religion, while gaining whatever is better in another. In that way, honour would be rendered to God, peace would be given to the peoples, and security to the empire' (Binyon, pp.130f.). It burst forth anew in Rousseau and Goethe, who believed that there was 'a basic religion, that of pure nature and reason, and that this is of divine origin' (*cf*. Hooft, p.26). And the same fundamental approach is shared by such men as W. E. Hocking and Arnold Toynbee. The latter rejects 'what he calls the "argument" of the Christian Church that it is unique in virtue of the uniqueness of Christ and of his incarnation. It is not credible that "God who is another name for love and who is believed to have demonstrated his love for Man by becoming incarnate in a human being, will have done this self-sacrificing deed of emptying himself at one time and place and one only." What remains are the teachings of Christianity. But these are not exclusively Christian. For the idea of God's self-sacrifice is found in ancient nature-worship and in Buddhism' (quoted in Hooft, pp.35f.).

Here the fundamental fallacy is that Hocking, Toynbee and a multitude of other writers tend to interpret Christianity 'wholly in terms of ideas', rather than God's decisive intervention in history. 'But Christianity is not a philosophical system; it is, as Lesslie Newbigin says, "primarily news and only secondarily views." (*A faith for this one World*, p.45.) And if the news is denied the views hang in the air' (Hooft, p.35).

There have been a number of recent manifestations of Syncretism also in the East – quite apart from the fact that Hinduism, and indeed many of the traditional religions of Africa and much of Asia, are syncretistic in their very nature. Thus the great Hindu mystic Rāmakrishna 'would speak of himself as the same soul that had been born before as Rāma, as Krishna, as Jesus or as Buddha'. His teachings were propagated by Swami Vivekānanda, who appealed, at the World's Parliament of Religions in Chicago in 1893, that those present should proclaim to the world that all paths lead to the same God, and who exclaimed: 'May he who is the Brahma of the Hindus, the Ahura Mazda of the Zoroastrians, the Buddha of the Buddhists, the Jehovah of the Jews, the Father in Heaven of the Christians, give strength to you to carry out your noble idea' (*cf.* Hooft, pp.36ff.).

It was thus that Gandhi insisted that 'The need of the moment is not one religion, but mutual respect and tolerance of the different religions.... Any attempt to root out traditions, effects of heredity, etc., is not only bound to fail, but is a sacrilege. The soul of religions is one, but it is encased in a multitude of forms. The latter will persist to the end of time... Truth is the exclusive property of no single scripture... I cannot ascribe exclusive divinity to Jesus. He is as divine as Krishna or Rama or Mahomed or Zoroaster' (Dewick, p.20).

Syncretic sects and movements have burgeoned, in recent years, from the soil of many different religions. Such, from a Hindu background, are the Rāmakrishna Mission and the Theosophical movement, the aim of which is 'to rescue from degradation the archaic truths which are the basis of all religions; and to uncover the fundamental unity from which they all spring' (Blavatsky, Vol.1, p.viii). Such, too – from a Muslim origin – is Bahā'ism, for the nine doors through which men may enter the great Bahā'ī temple in Wilmette, near Chicago, represent the 'nine religions of the world', which all find in the Bahā'ī faith the essence of their own belief and the definitive revelation of ultimate reality. Syncretic movements can also be found in Japan, where the symbol of Ittoen, the Garden of Light, is a 'swastika with a cross at the centre and a sun in the background', and whose prayer is, 'Teach us to worship the essence of all religions, and help us to learn the one ultimate truth' (Hooft, pp.43,45). It is clear, moreover, that Spiritualism, in so far as it has been developed as a specific religious movement, has definitely syncretistic features. And Visser 't Hooft points out that even Moral Rearmament, by preaching 'change' without specifying the religious content of that change, contributes to the syncretistic confusion of our time (Hooft, p.48).

Syncretism, then, is a continually recurrent phenomenon. One of its comparatively recent apostles was, indeed, D. H. Lawrence, who himself described *Lady Chatterley's Lover* as 'frankly and faithfully a phallic novel', which seeks to resuscitate the spirit of the ancient fertility cults. But the acme of Lawrence's syncretism is to be found in *The Man Who Died*, where he goes so far as to depict the risen Christ as discovering true life when he embraces the priestess of the temple of Isis, and says, 'This is the great atonement, the being in touch. The gray sea and the rain, the wet narcissus and the woman I wait for, the invisible Isis and the unseen sun are all in touch and at one' (*The Man Who Died*, p.148).

Visser 't Hooft justly remarks that Syncretism, in many different forms, has the same basic motifs...Thus we hear a hundred times and in all languages that there are many ways to God and that God is too great,[4] too unknowable to reveal himself in a single revelation and once for all. Syncretism is thus essentially a revolt against the uniqueness of revelation in history. True universality, it claims, can only be gained if the pretension that God has actually made himself definitely known in a particular person and event at a particular time is given up. Now a God who speaks in an infinite variety of ways but never decisively really throws man back upon himself, for it is then up to man to determine how and where he can reach ultimate truth. Thus the syncretisms conceive of religion as a system of insights and concepts rather than as a dialogical relation between a personal God and his creature. They all tend to some form of gnosis, sometimes of a more rationalistic kind, sometimes more intuitive or esoteric. They seek to realize salvation rather than to receive it. In this way they are, often unwittingly, contradicting their own claim to universality. For they in fact exclude those religions for which the revelation of a personal God is the central category (Hooft, pp.48f.).

In this quest for ultimate truth Lesslie Newbigin emphasizes what Nicol Macnicol calls 'the great divide among the religions': namely, their attitude to history. 'There are in principle two ways in which one can seek unity and coherence behind or beyond all the multiplicity and incoherence which human experience presents to us. One way is to seek unity as an existent reality behind the multiplicity of phenomena...' – and this, Newbigin says, is typified in the wheel.

The cycle of birth, growth, decay and death through which plants, animals, human beings and institutions all pass suggests the rotating wheel – ever in movement yet ever returning upon itself. The wheel offers a way of escape from this endless and meaningless movement. One can find a way to the centre where all is still, and one

---

[4] Although not in the writings of men such as D. H. Lawrence and J. M. Allegro.

can observe the ceaseless movement without being involved in it. There are many spokes connecting the circumference with the centre. The wise man will not quarrel about which spoke should be chosen. Any one will do, provided it leads to the centre. Dispute among the different 'ways' of salvation is pointless; all that matters is that those who follow them should find their way to that timeless, motionless centre where all is peace, and where one can understand all the endless movement and change which makes up human history – understand that it goes nowhere and means nothing (*The Finality of Christ*, pp.65f.).

Here, many believe, we can discern the shadowy image of the world religion of the future. Thus Lawrence Hyde writes: 'Amidst all the conflicts and confusions, the sympathetic observer can trace the emerging outlines of a new form of religion ... what may prove to be the ground-plan of the Temple in which our spiritual descendants are destined to worship. The structure which thus discloses itself is *absolutely fundamental* – that of that Wisdom Religion which *by a metaphysical necessity* must provide the interior key to all exterior symbolisations and observances. It is the Way which leads back to Origin and it follows "the Pattern of the Cross"' (*The Wisdom Religion Today*, as quoted in Dewick, p.19). But E. C. Dewick points out that this last phrase does not refer to the cross as interpreted in historic Christianity, for L. Hyde continues: 'The great majority of those who are finding their way back to religion, from scepticism and materialism, are not returning to the faith of their fathers, but to some form of Wisdom Religion ... The Neo-Gnostic interprets the Incarnation as a process everlastingly being accomplished within the souls of all men and women; and from this he derives a wonderful sense of exaltation; it enables him to feel mystically one with every child of God.'

But the fundamental fact about the incarnation is that it was a unique, historical event in which God himself intervened decisively in the world he had created. It is precisely at this point that the Christian must of necessity part company with a great deal that is included under the comprehensive umbrella of Mysticism. This phenomenon is found in so many different religions – and is, indeed, often expressed in such similar terms – that it frequently appears as an emotional or intuitive form of Syncretism. As such, it must briefly engage our attention later in this chapter. But first we must cast a brief glance at the other side of Macnicol's 'great divide' – the symbol of which, Newbigin tells us, is not a wheel but a road. Life is a journey, a pilgrimage. 'The movement in which we are involved is not meaningless movement; it is movement towards a goal.' And along that road there lie a whole succession of historical events: chief among which are, of course, the incarnation, the cross and the resurrection. There are, moreover, innumerable points at which the traveller must choose between two or more alternative paths. And the 'goal, the ultimate resting-place, the experience of coherence and harmony, is not to be had save at the end of the road. The perfect goal is not a timeless reality hidden now behind the multiplicity and change which we experience; it is yet to be achieved; it lies at the end of the road' (*The Finality of Christ*, p.66).

It will have been noticed that in the preceding pages we have wandered, almost inevitably, from Syncretism in its strict sense to the wider context in which that same term is so frequently used. But it will make for greater clarity, I think, if we now turn decisively to what I have termed Religious Pluralism.

Religious Pluralism or the Universe of Faiths

In this connection I shall concentrate chiefly on two or three recent books by John Hick, on Hans Küng's magisterial presentation of a distinctly avant-garde Roman Catholic approach, and on a brief reply to both authors in a recent publication by Lesslie Newbigin to which I shall refer frequently in later chapters of this book. I have chosen Hick as an outstanding example of those radical scholars who approach this subject in a way that seems to meet with wider acceptance today than does that of Syncretism in the strict meaning of that term. So I shall attempt briefly to summarize his thesis.

First, Hick very naturally revolts against the traditional Roman Catholic doctrine that was expressed at the Council of Florence (1438–45), for example, in the declaration that 'The holy Roman Church believes, professes and proclaims that none of those who are outside the Church – not only pagans, but Jews also, heretics and schismatics – can have part in eternal life, but will go to the eternal fire "which was prepared for the devil and his angels", unless they are gathered into that Church before the end of life' (*cf.* Hans Küng, *On Being a Christian*, p.97). He recognizes, of course, that in practice there are very few people who would accept this view today; and elsewhere he quotes the wholly different emphasis of Vatican II, where the Dogmatic Constitution of the Church, promulgated in 1964, states that

> Those also can attain to everlasting salvation who through no fault of their own do not know the gospel of Christ or His Church, yet sincerely seek God and, moved by grace, strive by their deeds to do His will as it is known to them through the dictates of conscience. Nor does divine Providence deny the help necessary for salvation to those who, without blame on their part, have not yet arrived at an explicit knowledge of God, but who strive to live a good life, thanks to His grace. Whatever goodness or truth is found among them is looked upon by the Church as a preparation for the Gospel (Ch. ii, para. 16. *Cf.* Hick, *God and the Universe of Faiths*, pp.125f.).

He similarly revolts against what he describes as the 'Protestant missionary equivalent' of the traditional Roman Catholic dogma that there is 'no salvation outside the Church' – namely, the doctrine that there is 'no salvation outside Christianity' – as expressed as recently as 1960 in the declaration of the Congress on World Mission at Chicago that

> In the years since the war, more than one billion souls have passed into eternity and more than half of these went to the torment of hell fire without even hearing of

Jesus Christ, who He was, or why He died on the cross of Calvary (Percy, *Facing the Unfinished Task*, p.9).

But again Hick comments that this statement would be 'entertained by few today' (*God Has Many Names*, p.49).

Secondly, he notes a number of ways in which Christians have sought to 're-interpret' such statements as theologically untenable *per se* – and especially so in a situation in which all those who profess to be Christians represent only about a quarter of the world's population, in which converts from some other religions are comparatively rare, and in which millions have had no real opportunity to hear (or, still less, to understand) the gospel. So

in the attempt to retain the dogma of no salvation outside the Church, or outside Christianity, we have the ideas of implicit, as distinguished from explicit, faith; of baptism by desire, as distinguished from literal baptism; and, as a Protestant equivalent, the idea of a latent Church as distinguished from the manifest Church; and, again, the suggestion that men can only come to God through Jesus Christ but that those who have not encountered him in this life will encounter him in the life to come (*God Has Many Names*, p.50).

Somewhat similarly, there is 'Karl Rahner's notion of the anonymous Christian', which Hick describes as 'an honorary status granted unilaterally to people who have not expressed any desire for it'! Yet again, he continues, 'there is Hans Küng's distinction between the "ordinary" way of salvation in the world religions and the "extra-ordinary" way in the church'. But I must allow Küng to express this distinction in his own words:

A man is to be saved within the religion that is made available to him in his historical situation. Hence it is his right and his duty to seek God within that religion in which the hidden God has already found him. All this until such time as he is confronted in an existential way with the revelation of Jesus Christ. The religions . . . are *the way of salvation* in universal salvation history; the general way of salvation, we can even say, for the people of the world's religions: the more common, the '*ordinary*' way of salvation, as against which the way of salvation in the Church appears as something very special and extraordinary (Neuner, pp.52f.).[5]

Hick describes this approach as, at first sight, 'extremely promising'. But he objects that Küng then 'goes on to take away with one hand what he has given with the other', since 'the ordinary way of salvation for the majority of mankind in the world religions turns out to be only an interim way until, sooner or later, they come to an explicit Christian faith'. In the interim they are, in Küng's words, 'pre-Christian, directed towards Christ', since, by the grace of God, 'they are called and marked out to be Christians'[6] (*God Has Many Names*, pp.50f.).

Thirdly, and as a result of his repudiation of what he describes as the traditional doctrines that there is 'no salvation outside the Church' or 'outside Christianity' (and his dissatisfaction with the various attempts which have been made by what Küng has described as a 'pseudo-orthodox stretching of the meaning of Christian concepts like "Church" and "salvation"' to soften, or widen, these dogmas), Hick proposes 'A shift from the dogma that Christianity is at the centre to the *realisation* that it is God who is at the centre' (*God and the Universe of Faiths*, p.131). He seems to have got this notion primarily from Wilfred Cantwell Smith's *The Meaning and End of Religion*, the originality of which (as Hick puts it, in his Foreword to its publication in Britain in 1978) lies in the distinction he makes between

> two different realities, which he calls faith and the cumulative traditions, these being the inner and outer aspects of man's religious life. What he calls faith . . . is an individual's, or many individuals', relationship with the divine Transcendent, whether the latter be known as personal or as non-personal, as one or many, as moral or as non-moral, as gracious or as demanding . . . . All this is

---

[5] Küng's views are, however, much more adequately expressed in his magisterial work *On Being a Christian* (A III, pp.57–112). Yet, with respect, fundamental weaknesses still (I am convinced) remain.   [6] *On Being a Christian*, p.98.

an immediate, inner, personal, living and 'existential' participation in an experienced relationship with the greater, perhaps infinitely greater, and mysterious reality which in English we call God.... The cumulative traditions, as distinct from inner personal faith, are problem areas in the quite different ways in which history is always in varying degrees problematic (*The Meaning and End of Religion*, pp.xivf.).

It was the perception of this perfectly valid distinction between what I would term the 'subjective' faith of individuals or groups and the 'objective traditions' by which they have been conditioned that had the effect of setting Hick free, it seems, 'to develop, in *God and the Universe of Faiths*, the idea of a "Copernican revolution" in our theology of religions, consisting in a paradigm shift from a Christianity-centred or Jesus-centred to a God-centred model of the universe of faiths. One then sees the great world religions as different human responses to the one divine Reality, embodying different perceptions which have been formed in different historical and cultural circumstances' (*God Has Many Names*, pp.5f.).

Hick realizes, of course, that 'this paradigm shift' must necessarily involve 'a re-opening of the Christological question'. This is obviously true, and leads Hick at once into his familiar groove.

For if Jesus was literally God incarnate, the Second Person of the Holy Trinity living a human life, so that the Christian religion was founded by God-on-earth in person, it is then very hard to escape from the traditional view that all mankind must be converted to the Christian faith. However, the alternative possibility suggests itself that the idea of divine incarnation is to be understood metaphorically rather than literally, as an essentially poetic expression of the Christian's devotion to his lord. As such, it should not be treated as a metaphysical truth from which we can draw further conclusions, such as that God's saving activity is confined to the single thread of human history documented in the Christian Bible (*God Has Many Names*, pp.5f.).

Each of these points will, of course, demand comment in the course of this book; but it seems illogical and misleading to attempt to take such a number of very heterogeneous hurdles in the span of one breathless gallop. If the hurdles are to be taken seriously, they must surely be considered on their merits, each in its proper place. So I shall revert to the explicit terms of the apostolic proclamation about Jesus, right from the beginning of the Christian mission, in chapter 2; to the unique relationship that Jesus habitually claimed with his Father, whom (he said) he alone could fully reveal to men, in chapter 4; and to the meaning, source and scope of true 'salvation' in chapters 3, 5 and 6. But there are three points that should, perhaps, be made at once.

A few general remarks

First, it is clear that Hick certainly does not support a syncretistic approach to the world's religions, if one takes the term Syncretism in its narrower sense. He does not advocate any attempt to fuse the different religious traditions which are so deeply entrenched in our very varied cultures. On the contrary, he positively delights in the richness of their diversity. 'What we are picturing here as a future possibility', he writes,

> is not a single world religion, but a situation in which the different traditions no longer see themselves and each other as rival ideological communities. A single world religion is, I would think, never likely, and not a consummation to be desired. For so long as there is a variety of human types there will be a variety of kinds of worship and a variety of theological emphases and approaches. There will always be the more mystical and the more prophetic types of faith, with the corresponding awareness of the ultimate Reality as non-personal and as personal. There will always be the more spontaneous, warm and Spirit-filled forms of devotion, and the more liturgical, orderly and rationally controlled forms (*God Has Many Names*, p.58).

Now it is certainly true that men and women will always be richly diversified in their qualities of heart and mind, for nature itself declares with one voice that God loves variety. So there will always be differences – and, no doubt, degrees – in the way in which human beings apprehend, approach and worship God – or, indeed, reject him, flee from him or deny his existence. It is only when his redeemed people, from 'every tribe and language, people and nation' are at last perfected, that we shall *corporately* be able to grasp 'what is the breadth and length and height and depth, and to know the love of Christ which surpasses knowledge' (Eph. 3:18f.). But are we really to believe, in the meantime, that the 'Transcendent Reality' can be both personal and non-personal, and that he (or it?) can combine qualities which are not only bewilderingly varied but diametrically contradictory – even, as Cantwell Smith puts it, both 'moral' and 'non-moral' or (to be brutally frank) good, kind, loving and beautiful and also, at the same time, evil, malignant, cruel and revolting? I could perhaps in *theory* – although not, I think, in practice – believe that there is no Transcendent Reality at all, but that human beings are so constituted that they feel compelled to postulate some ultimate Being or Power (whom they then conceive or depict in terms of their own characters, propensities and aspirations). Naturally enough, in that case, the resultant figments of their collective imaginations would include a certain degree of coherence coupled with startling contradictions. But what I can certainly *not* believe is that a Transcendent Reality like this really exists, or could possibly have 'revealed himself' in such wholly incongruous terms.

Secondly, much has been written about the attitude that Christians should take to other religions as such, and to this we must return in rather more detail in chapter 5. What primarily concerns us at this point is how we view the Christian faith in this pluralistic setting. Hick is absolutely right when he makes it clear (p.26, above) that the basic criterion is whether we are convinced by all the evidence that Jesus really was (as the early church indubitably believed and the apostles unequivocally proclaimed) God-in-manhood: no mere theophany, but a genuine incarnation in which the eternal God became man 'for us men and for our salvation'. To the apostolic church this was proved not only by the hitherto unparalleled intimacy of the way in which he habitually conversed with God as 'Abba, my own Father' and spoke to men with the authority of God himself, but pre-eminently by the fact that – contrary to all their expectations – God had raised him from the dead and exalted him to his right hand, to the very throne of the universe. It was from this time that they began, instinctively it seems, to call him 'Lord Jesus' or simply 'Lord'; that they felt at liberty – and even compelled – to worship him; that they frequently applied to him Old Testament verses originally addressed to (or descriptive of) Yahweh, their covenant God; and that they sometimes invoked him directly in prayer.

Before the resurrection the disciples had already come to believe that their Master was the promised Messiah, although he seems studiously to have avoided using this title in his public preaching. They had also dimly perceived his unique relationship with the Father. But it was the empty tomb and the series of resurrection appearances that convinced them that, by this divine act, he had been openly and unmistakably 'declared to be the Son of God with power' (Rom. 1:4, AV), and that one day 'every tongue [should] confess that Jesus Christ is Lord, to the glory of God the Father' (Phil. 2:11). And the resurrection also convinced them of another fundamental fact: that his death on the cross 'in weakness' had really been his glory (*cf.* Jn. 12:27f.; 13:31f.; Gal. 6:14). Basically, it had not been the death of a great reformer who proclaimed a message his contempories had not been ready to receive, but rather – as he himself had said it would be – 'a ransom for many' (Mk. 10:45), the 'blood of the covenant, . . . poured out for many for the forgiveness of sins' (Mt. 26:28). The earliest tradition on this subject was 'that Christ died for our sins in accordance with the scriptures' (1 Cor. 15:3); and the apostolic conclusion was that he, in his atoning death, was (and is) 'the propitiation for our sins, and not only for ours but also for the sins of the whole world' (1 Jn. 2:2).

Thirdly, the fact is that Christology and soteriology cannot be divided. This is true on at least two distinct grounds. To begin with, it is only the fact of who Christ was that gave his sacrificial death its redemptive and atoning significance; for unless there had been an essential unity of being between the Father who sent and the Son who came, it would not have been possible for Paul to proclaim that 'God demonstrates his own love for us in this: While we were still sinners, Christ died for us' (Rom. 5:8). Then again, our need for redemption is no less than our need for revelation, although it is on the latter that comparisons between different religions commonly concentrate. It is, of course, of supreme importance that we should know God as he really is (Jn. 17:3); but how could any revelation avail us until the sin that inevitably blinds our eyes had been effectively dealt with and we had been 'reconciled' to him? It is only when 'justified by faith' that sinful men and women can 'have peace with God' and enjoy 'access' to his grace; and it is deeply significant that the 'New Covenant' of inward transformation (with the 'law' of God written on our hearts and minds rather than on two external tablets of stone challenging our unwilling obedience) should not only lead us deeper and deeper into a personal knowledge of God, but find its very foundation in a full and free forgiveness (Heb. 8:8–12).

The means of 'salvation'

It is pre-eminently in this respect that all religions, as such, betray their basic inadequacy, since we must insist that religion in itself – even Christianity – is *never* the means of salvation. The reason for this is that no human being can be 'saved' by the quality of his life, the rigour of his asceticism, the fervency of his devotions, or the orthodoxy of his convictions; for it remains true that all of us, without exception, have sinned and continually fall short of the only standard that a holy God must require. It is only when we come, spiritually naked, to the cross where God himself, in the man Christ Jesus, revealed not only sin as it really is but also the love which prompted him to go to such an incredible length to redeem men (whatever their condition) and to extend to them all the riches of his grace, that we realize that there is, in fact, no other way. As Stephen Neill once put it: 'For the human sickness there is one specific remedy, and this is it. There is no other' (Neill, p.94). Or, in the words of Lesslie Newbigin:

> This unique historic deed, which we confess as the true turning point of universal history, stands throughout history as witness against all the claims of religion – including the Christian religion – to be the means of salvation. . . . The message of Jesus, of the unique incarnate Lord crucified by the powers of law, morals and piety and raised to the throne of cosmic authority, confronts every religion with a radical negation. We cannot escape this (*The Open Secret*, p.200).

Elsewhere he makes this same point when he insists that:

> Down the centuries, from the first witness until today, the church has sought and used innumerable symbols to express the inexpressible mystery of the event which is the centre, the crisis of all cosmic history, the hinge upon which all happenings turn. Christ the sacrifice offered for our sin, Christ the substitute standing in our place, Christ the ransom price paid for our redemption, Christ the conqueror casting out the prince of this world – these and other symbols have been used to point to the heart of the mystery. None can fully express it (*The Open Secret*, p.56).

But these categorical statements about the one and only 'specific remedy' for 'the human sickness' and the 'unique historic deed, which we confess as the true turning point of universal history', do not of themselves *exclude* anyone, except those who with open eyes persist in rejecting them. Even within the favoured 'Judaeo-Christian tradition', to which Hick so frequently refers, one cannot really assert that Abraham, Moses or David, for example – to say nothing of the multitude of simple Old Testament believers – had any clear understanding of what God was going to do, centuries later, not by any animal sacrifice that they brought (in their obedience and faith), but in the Son of his love, in whom he was himself present and active. Yet the New Testament is emphatic that it was to this supreme sacrifice that they in fact owed their salvation (*cf.* Rom. 3:25; Heb. 9:15). In a later chapter I raise the possibility that, where the 'God of all grace' has been at work by his Spirit in the hearts of individuals from other religious backgrounds, revealing to them something of their sin and need and enabling them (as he alone can) to throw themselves on his mercy, they too may profit from this 'specific remedy' for man's spiritual sickness and this 'unique historic deed' which still stands as 'the turning point of history', but about which they have never had the opportunity to hear (*cf.* pp.145–155, below).

If this is true there is no need whatever to fabricate a category of 'anonymous Christians', or to indulge in 'a pseudo-orthodox stretching of the meaning of Christian concepts like "Church" and "salvation",' in order to 'soften' the affirmation that salvation is in and through Jesus alone, and that 'there is no other name under heaven given to men by which we must be saved' (Acts 4:12). This statement stands: the only question is, who is included in this salvation? To quote Newbigin again, 'the revelation of God's saving love and power in Jesus entitles and requires me to believe that God purposes the salvation of all men,[7] but it does not entitle me to believe that this purpose is to be accomplished in any way which ignores or bypasses the historic event by which it was in fact revealed and effected' (*The Open Secret*, pp.200f.). Nor do these facts drive us to believe in an indiscriminate Universalism (as Hick's views clearly do). We should all rejoice if this were true, but the Bible seems to me decisively to preclude any such conclusion.

What is clear, I think, is that we dare not dogmatize about the ultimate salvation of others. To say this is emphatically *not* to dismiss the problem, as Küng alleges that Protestant theologians do, 'with a supercilious "we don't know" as if it were no concern of theirs' (*On Being a Christian*, p.99). On the contrary, it is to let God be God, with Abraham's assurance: 'Shall not the Judge of all the earth do right?' (Gn. 18:25). It is in this context that Newbigin pertinently observes that 'In the many references

---

[7] *Cf.* 1 Tim. 2:4; 2 Pet. 3:9. This is what God in his love '*wills*' for all; but the verse does not assert that this is a divine 'purpose' which he will bring to completion regardless of man's response. Newbigin, I know, is in total agreement with this footnote.

to final judgment in the teaching of Jesus, the most characteristic feature is the emphasis on the element of surprise'
(*The Open Secret*, p.88). The humble penitent is over-
whelmed with joy and gratitude, while the self-confident
professor is dumbfounded (*cf*. p.147, below).

It is precisely here that Küng (let alone Hick) gives one
pause. Küng, for example, suggests 'that non-Christians
too *as observers of the law* can be justified' (*On Being a
Christian*, p.91. My italics); and that 'the other religions' are
'legitimate religions' because they provide 'forms of belief
and worship, concepts and values, symbols and ordinances,
religious and ethical experiences, which have a "relative
validity"'. But surely this adds up to something much more
reminiscent of the attitude of the legally observant and
ceremonially meticulous Pharisee than that of the tax-
collector, of whom Jesus said that 'It was this man,...and
not the other, who went home acquitted of his sins' (Lk.
18:14, NEB). Hick, again, refers almost in one breath to 'the
early Jewish prophets'; to Zoroaster in Persia; to Lao-tzu
and Confucius in China; to the Upanishads, 'Gotama the
Buddha', 'Mahivira, the founder of the Jain religion', and
the Bhagavad Gītā in India; to Pythagoras, Socrates and
Plato in Greece; and 'then, after a gap of some three hundred
years', to 'Jesus of Nazareth and the emergence of Christianity' and (after another gap) to 'the prophet Mohammed
and the rise of Islam' (*God and the Universe of Faiths*,
pp.125f.).

Küng, it is true, faithfully refers to the differences as well
as the similarities between the great religions (*cf*. *On Being
a Christian*, pp.100ff. with p.92) and observes, even in
regard to 'archetypal men', that 'they stand beside each
other disparately.... Only a naive ignorance of the facts
makes it possible to overlook or assimilate the distinctive
qualities of each one. A decision can scarcely be avoided'
(p.103). Hick, on the other hand, blandly suggests that we
should consider the persons and books on his list as all
representing 'moments of divine revelation', and observes
that, at the time concerned, 'it was not possible for God to
reveal himself through any human mediation to all mankind'. This is clearly true, and explains why it seems always
to have been God's plan to entrust those to whom he has

progressively revealed himself with the responsibility of going and telling others. But it certainly does not entitle us to believe that authentic divine revelations would – or could – be mutually (and sometimes diametrically) contradictory.

Küng himself lists some such examples. *Inter alia*, he emphasizes the 'substantial differences... between a religion whose symbol is the lingam (stone phallus), reproduced a thousandfold in the same temple, and another whose symbol is the cross; between a religion proclaiming a holy war against the enemy and a religion which makes love of enemies an essential part of its program; between a religion of human sacrifice (at least twenty thousand human beings sacrificed within four days at the consecration of the main temple in Mexico in 1487) and a religion of everyday self-sacrifice for man. Even the cruelties of the Spanish *conquistadors* and the Roman burning of heretics – not in fact in accordance with the Christian scheme but contradicting it, not Christian but unequivocally anti-Christian – do not cancel out these differences' (*On Being a Christian*, p.102). Surely, then, Newbigin is right when he insists that 'there is light and there is darkness. But light shines on the darkness to the uttermost; there is no point at which light stops and darkness begins, unless the light has been put under a bushel. When the light shines freely one cannot draw a line and say, "Here light stops and darkness begins." But one can and must say, "*There* is where the light shines; go towards it and your path will be clear; turn your back on it and you will go into deeper darkness"' (*The Open Secret*, pp.197f.). One can, moreover, add with confidence that *that* Light will never be put out; and I am convinced that we can also rest assured that those who genuinely throw themselves on the mercy, love and faithfulness of God will be given the grace to persevere, or 'stand fast to the end' (*cf.* Mt. 10:22; 24:13).

A brief comparison of attitudes

Before we turn to Mysticism, it may be appropriate to attempt briefly to summarize the basic differences between the attitudes of Newbigin, Küng and Hick on this subject.

The quotations I have given from Newbigin largely, I think, speak for themselves – although his stance will become increasingly clear in subsequent chapters of this book. He has had a long and intimate experience of cross-cultural witness and inter-faith relations; and while he is prepared to answer the question 'Is there a real communion between God and the believer in non-Christian religious experience?' with 'a plain affirmative' (*cf. The Finality of Christ*, p.38), he, like R. Panikkar (*cf.* pp.36, 172f., below), firmly believes that 'Christ is the universal redeemer; no one is saved unless it be by him' (*ibid.*, p.41). Yet he cannot, for at least two reasons, go along with Panikkar's statement that 'The good and bona fide Hindu is saved by Christ and not by Hinduism, but it is through the sacraments of Hinduism, through the message of morality and the good life, through the mysterion that comes down to him through Hinduism, that Christ saves the Hindu normally' (*The Unknown Christ of Hinduism*, p.54).

The first reason why Newbigin cannot endorse this statement is because he objects (rightly, as I see it) to Panikkar's emphasis here on the 'good' Hindu, since it is of the essence of the gospel that Jesus came 'not to call the righteous, but sinners'. And the second reason is that Newbigin insists that 'The focus of the Gospel is the word [or judgment] of the Cross' (*The Finality of Christ*, p.57), as the unique and 'decisive encounter of God with men – not just with men as individual "souls" detachable from their place in human history, but with mankind as a whole, with human history as a whole, indeed with the whole creation' (*ibid.*, p.49). So

To be saved is to participate – in foretaste now and in fulness at the end – in this final victory of Christ. According to the New Testament, the coming of Christ, his dying and rising and ascension, is the decisive moment in God's plan of salvation, presenting to every man who hears it the opportunity and the necessity for faith, repentance, conversion and commitment to participation in the work of God in this present age. It is certainly made clear that it is possible to refuse this opportunity and thereby to lose the possibility of salvation – to be lost. But it is not, I believe, implied that the vast multitudes who have never been presented with this Gospel call for conversion and commitment are thereby necessarily excluded from participation in God's on-going and completed work (*ibid.*, p.61).

What precise attitude would Küng take to all this, I wonder? I do not feel that my acquaintance with, or understanding of, his theological position gives me the right to be in any way dogmatic on this subject. It is certainly clear that, with all his concessions to 'the religions', he believes God's revelation in Christ to stand on a pinnacle by itself as uniquely true. 'If Christian theology today asserts that all men – even in the world religions – *can* be saved', he writes, 'this certainly does not mean that all religions are equally true. They will be saved, not because of, but in spite of polytheism, magic, human sacrifice, forces of nature. They will be saved, not because of, but in spite of all untruth and superstition' (*On Being a Christian*, p.104. My italics). What he does not make at all clear here is why they will be saved. Unlike Panikkar, he does not, in this context, make any unequivocal statement that salvation for all men can ultimately be through Christ (and what God did in him at the cross) *alone*. But later in his book his emphasis on the centrality of the cross is more explicit, at least for believers. In regard to the apostle Paul, for example, he writes: 'To put it briefly and epigrammatically, the Christian message is the word of the cross. It is a word which may not be cancelled or emptied of meaning, nor may it be suppressed or mythicized. . . . This crucified and living Jesus then is for believers the foundation which is already laid and which cannot be replaced by any other. The Crucified as living is the ground of faith. He is the criterion of freedom' (*ibid.*, pp.399f.).

There was a day when Hick, as he tells us himself, would have been even more unequivocal (*cf. God Has Many Names*, pp.2ff.). But those days have long since passed. Even when, in 1968, he published *Christianity at the Centre*, he tells us that the title 'was deliberately ambiguous, suggesting either the centre or essence of Christianity, or Christianity at the centre of life or at the centre of the universe of faiths'. But 'this latter interpretation would be misleading', he explains, in the light of the way in which his mind had been moving in the intervening years, and this new version, published in 1977 as *The Centre of Christianity*, has additional sections which explain the conclusions to which he has now come regarding 'the relation between Christianity and the other world religions and the place of Jesus Christ in this wider religious scene' (pp.7f.). What these conclusions are may be gathered, in part, from what I have already written and from a number of passages later in this book. Suffice it in this context, therefore, to say that he is now a Pluralist who stands apart from Küng – and much further still, of course, from Newbigin.

Mysticism

Mysticism is a comprehensive word which means different things to different people. In general terms it represents the belief that direct knowledge of God, of spiritual truth or ultimate reality, is attainable 'through immediate intuition or insight and in a way differing from ordinary sense perception or the use of logical reasoning' (*Webster's New Collegiate Dictionary*). Broadly speaking, there seem to be two main types of mysticism. The one is essentially introvertive, in which the mystic 'by turning inwards on his own consciousness and experience, and by stressing the necessity for discarding from his mind all visual or concrete images, comes to realise in a peculiarly coercive way his essential oneness with ultimate reality' (E. J. Tinsley, 'Mysticism', p.226). The other, which may be termed extrovertive, is 'closely akin to the experience of the poet and the prophet', and is linked with some objective experience or circumstance – or with what the early Christian Fathers called the 'mystery'.

This second type of mysticism may, it is clear, be distinctively Christian. In the early church it seems that mystical experience was almost always associated with something factual or concrete; *e.g.* with the written words of Scripture or the action of the liturgy. 'The sign, the concrete event or situation, or piece of Scripture, and the thing signified were taken as inseparable. This patristic type of mysticism is a genuine mysticism and at the same time is completely compatible with Christian belief in an historical incarnation' (Tinsley, p.225).

But the reason why mysticism must concern us in this context is the close connection that it can have with both Syncretism and Pluralism (which, as we have seen, are closely related). This is partly because mystics, from whatever religion or background they come, are apt to speak the same sort of language, and partly because mystics in different religious traditions often recognize in each other a common experience which, they assert, transcends their theological differences. So the question inevitably arises as to whether this phenomenon does in fact provide evidence for an ultimate reality which lies behind the formulations of all religions and represents the truth that they are all trying, however imperfectly, to proclaim. How otherwise can we account for the evidence, from so many different traditions, of mystical experiences which, however much they may differ in form and depth, seem – at first sight, at least – recognizably to belong to the same family or genus?

Part of the explanation of this phenomenon assuredly lies in the philosophy and discipline which mystics from different religions often have in common. Thus in the field with which I am myself best acquainted – Muslim mysticism – we find that Neo-platonic concepts (or Neo-platonic concepts popularized by the pseudo 'Dionysius the Areopagite') provide the basic philosophy and technique, and that this is often combined with a pantheistic or monistic pattern of thought which emanates from India. Thus the mystic fervently aspires to wean his heart and mind from the phenomenal world and to realize his unity with the Infinite.

It is also important to note what has been termed 'The unbroken line of continuity in the history of "provoked mysticism"' or techniques designed to induce states of mystical consciousness. To attain such states men have 'willingly submitted themselves to elaborate ascetic procedures...They have practised fasting, flagellation, and sensory deprivation, and, in so doing, may have attained to states of heightened mystical consciousness, but also have succeeded in altering their body chemistry.

Recent physiological investigations . . . tend to confirm the notion that provoked alterations in body chemistry and body rhythm are in no small way responsible for the dramatic changes in consciousness attendant upon these practices' (Masters and Houston, pp.248f.). Muslim dervishes, for example, have regularly attained an ecstatic state, or at least a condition of auto-hypnosis, by controlled breathing, regulated rhythm, chanting, dancing, whirling or the long maintenance of profound concentration. Similarly, devotees of both Yoga and Zen Buddhism meticulously follow their respective systems of posture, breathing and meditation.[8]

Drugs of various sorts have also been used for such purposes for centuries. Such may, indeed, have been the nature of the *soma* of the Vedic sacrifice[9]; such is the *peyote* of the Mazatec Indians of Mexico, Indian tribes in the United States and Canada and even of the 'Native American Church'[1]; and such, according to R. G. Wassan, is a hallucinogenic mushroom known in South America, among shamanistic tribes in Siberia, and elsewhere[2] – while derivatives of hemp, datura, henbane, *etc.*, have been still more widely used (Masters and Houston, pp.37ff.). More recently, 'the historic sacrality of the visionary vegetables has . . . given way to the modern notoriety of the synthetic derivatives – especially LSD, psilocybin, and mescaline' (Masters and Houston, p.252).

It was the publication of Aldous Huxley's *Doors of Perception* in 1954 which first popularized the use of what we may term psychedelic drugs for such purposes. There can be no doubt that while these drugs often induce a psychotic experience of panic, terror, paranoid distrust,

[8] *Cf.* E. G. Parrinder, *An Introduction to Asian Religions*, pp.47, 123; R. C. Zaehner, *Mysticism, Sacred and Profane*, pp.55, 95, 138, *etc.* Compare also the *kīrtan*, or rhythmical singing of hymns (sometimes to the accompaniment of dancing) in some Hindu sects of *bhakti* persuasion.
[9] R. C. Zaehner, *op. cit.*, p.3; Masters and Houston, p.250.
[1] *Cf.* R. C. Zaehner, *op. cit.*, pp.23f.; Masters and Houston, pp.39ff. In this Church a pagan rite has been given a 'Christian' form and expression.
[2] Masters and Houston, pp.250f., *etc.* But the properties of the fly agaric mushroom (*Amanita muscaria*) seem to have been much exaggerated by Wassan, and to have become an obsession with Allegro (*The Sacred Mushroom and the Cross*). There is no evidence at all, it seems, that this mushroom has ever grown in Judaea or the neighbourhood of Qumran, while a botanist at the Royal Botanical Gardens at Kew has stated that 'for its use as an inspiration for writers, philosophers or even rabble-rousers in Western Asia there is not one particle of evidence'.

delusions, toxic confusion and depression, they can also be used to uncover what is termed psychodynamic material from a patient's unconscious mind (Pahnke, pp.60ff.). They also sometimes have what may be called a *cognitive* or *aesthetic* effect, the former characterized by particularly lucid thought and the latter by increased sensory perception, although the records of what patients actually say when under the influence of these drugs seem to substantiate the latter much more than the former – or a riot of aesthetic stimuli rather than any lucidity of rational thought. But the problem, in this context, is whether or not these drugs may also stimulate transcendental or mystical experience.

A reasonably convincing case can be made out for the fact that experimental psychedelic experiences *sometimes* seem to betray the seven common characteristics of introvertive mystical states of mind which W. T. Stace tabulates as evidenced by a wide sampling of the literature of mystical experience.[3] These are (1) a Unitary Consciousness, or 'a sense of cosmic oneness through positive ego transcendence' (Pahnke, p.63); (2) a sense of being 'non-spatial and non-temporal', or the transcendence of space and time; (3) a sense of 'objectivity or reality'; (4) feelings of 'blessedness, joy, peace, happiness, *etc.*'; (5) a feeling that what is apprehended is 'holy, sacred or divine'; (6) paradoxicality; (7) an allegation that what they experience is 'ineffable' and impossible to describe – although Pahnke shrewdly observes that most of those who insist on this ineffability 'do in fact make elaborate attempts to communicate the experience'.[4] It is also sometimes alleged that these experiences, although themselves transient, result in 'positive changes in attitudes and behaviour'.

This may well be true. But the basic question, for the Christian, is what is the origin and source of these mystical experiences, whether they are spontaneous, aided or provoked by ascetic practices, or even induced by hallucinogenic vegetables or drugs. But this must largely depend on what the mystic is primarily concerned to

[3] W. T. Stace, *Mysticism and Philosophy*, pp.110f., as quoted by Masters and Houston, p.302.
[4] Contrast Paul in 2 Cor. 12:4.

achieve: is this to concentrate his attention on himself, on the phenomenal world (as in 'nature mysticism'), or on God? Here the first two categories of mysticism are united in being non-theistic, although sharply divided in so far as one is introverted and the other extroverted – with the result that they differ widely in their appropriate psychological techniques. But even those mystics whose ultimate aspiration is to know and enjoy God may themselves be subdivided into those who seek him through the medium of their own hearts, those who seek him through the medium of nature, and those who seek him directly, without any medium whatever. And it is significant, I think, that the great Christian mystical theologians – and, indeed, some of the leading Muslim *Ṣūfīs*[5] – would say that, in the highest mystical experience, any absorption with oneself or with nature must be no more than transitional stages to an exclusive concentration on God, and that any direct experience of him can never be reached by the mystic's own efforts, but only as a gift from God himself.

If, then, we ask what is the origin and source of mystical experiences – real or alleged – as a whole, the answer must be that an enormous proportion of them have their origin in the subconscious mind of the person concerned;[6] that they must sometimes be regarded as a Satanic delusion rather than any form of divine revelation (Masters and Houston, pp.39, 252); but that they are clearly sometimes of God – although I should myself be distinctly doubtful of this when they are chemically induced. It seems to me significant that while the rhapsodies of those under the influence of LSD or similar drugs often speak of ultimate reality, of cosmic unity, or sometimes of God (in very general or vividly aesthetic terms), even those who come from within the traditions of Christendom seldom speak in any meaningful way of the historic Christ.[7] But it is surely basic to true Christianity that it is only 'in the face of Jesus Christ' that the glory of God is *adequately* revealed. The

---

[5] *E.g.* al-Qushayrī, Junayd of Baghdad, *etc. Cf.* Zaehner, *Mysticism*, pp.85ff.

[6] *Cf.* Masters and Houston, p.256; Zaehner, *op. cit.*, pp.xv, 3, 39–41, 57, 59, 62, 92, *etc.*

[7] A *possible* exception to this may be found in the Native American Church. *Cf.* Masters and Houston, p.251.

great Christian mystics would themselves concur in emphasizing that Christian faith is firmly based on God's self-revelation in history, accepted in faith and repentance and translated into daily living, and that supernatural love (which can be known and enjoyed through the ordinary means of grace) is of much more importance than any mystical experience.

All the same, there are reasons other than those to which we have already referred which may explain, in part, how even mystics of the introvertive type often seem to speak somewhat the same language and to apprehend *something* of what the Christian finds in Christ. The first of these is that the mystic who 'turns inward on his own consciousness and experience' commonly believes that there, in his own heart, lies the 'image of God', ready for him to behold it, if only he can cleanse that heart – and, indeed, the eye with which he looks – from the dross of false values and from absorption in the material and the finite. And this is indeed, in some degree, perfectly true. As William Temple put it:

> Because man is made in the image of God, the attempt to find God through penetrating to the inmost recesses of the self leads in men of all times and races to a similar experience. God truly is the spring of life in our souls; so to seek that spring is to seek Him; and to find it would be to find Him. But this can never quite happen. The image of God in man is defaced by sin, that is by self-will. The mind which seeks to reach that image is distorted by sin, and moulded both for good and for evil by tradition. The *via negativa* of the mystics cannot be perfectly followed. To rely on a supposedly direct communion with God in detachment from all external aids is to expose the soul to suggestions arising from its distortion as well as to those arising from the God whom it would apprehend. Mediation there must be; imagery there must be. If we do not deliberately avail ourselves of the true Mediator, the 'express image' (Hebrews i, 3), we shall be at the mercy of some unworthy medium and of a distorted image (Temple, p.92).[8]

[8] *Cf.* also G. Campbell Morgan, *The Crises of the Christ*, pp.29ff.

In addition, before we can see God even in Christ we need the quickening and illumination of the Holy Spirit.

Yet again, we have already suggested (*cf.* pp.31f.) that, wherever and whenever the Spirit of God brings a man, whatever his religious background, to realize something of his sin or need, and to throw himself utterly on God's mercy, the Bible gives us reasons to believe that he will in fact find that mercy where it is always and only available – at the cross of Christ – and that he will be accepted and forgiven on the basis of what God himself did at that cross to make possible the forgiveness of the repentant sinner. If this is true, then it follows that those mystics from other religious traditions who have genuinely sought the face of God with a real sense of sin and need – as many of them undoubtedly have – have in all probability experienced his grace and forgiveness in Christ, little though they may have understood it. But this, by definition, applies to those whom R. C. Zaehner calls 'theistic' mystics rather than 'nature mystics' or even 'monistic mystics' (*Mysticism*, pp.28ff., 153ff.) – unless, of course, some of these in fact desert their own techniques and concepts and begin to seek God himself, or God directly intervenes and breaks through. But this is a controversial point to which further reference is made on pages 145–155, below.

The fact remains, however, that while 'mysticism as a system of practice and thought is central for India', it is 'marginal for Christianity' (Allen, p.110). Thus E. L. Allen, after quoting W. T. Stace's somewhat morbid summary of religion – 'the desire to break away from being and existence altogether, to get beyond existence into nothingness where the great light is. It is the desire to be utterly free from the fetters of being. For every being is a fetter. Existence is a fetter. To be is to be tied to what you are. Religion is the hunger for the non-being which yet is' (W. T. Stace, *Time and Eternity*, p.5) – pertinently asks what this has in common with the Sermon on the Mount or Wesley's hymns (Allen, p.111) – or, we might add, Paul's passionate desire 'to know Christ, to experience the power of his resurrection, and to share his sufferings, in growing conformity with his death' (Phil. 3:10, NEB). This fundamental Christian aspiration may, moreover, be interpreted both in terms of practical daily living and in those of truly Christian mysticism.

In true Christianity nothing can ever displace the concrete, historical figure of Jesus Christ from the central place. It is, indeed, significant that in Aldous Huxley's *Perennial Philosophy* the only form of Christianity which receives favourable mention is radical mysticism which, he says, 'went some way towards liberating Christianity from its unfortunate servitude to historic fact' and presents in its place 'a spiritualized and universalized Christianity'. He regrets, however, that even in it 'the pure Perennial Philosophy has been overlaid, now more, now less, by an idolatrous preoccupation with events and things... regarded not merely as useful means, but as ends, intrinsically sacred and indeed divine' (Huxley, p.63. *Cf.* Hooft, pp.89f.).

As for those mystics who go beyond all this and even claim that they have attained complete union, and identification, with God – such as Meister Eckhart and Angelus Silesius among Christians, and Abū Yazīd, Hallāj and several others among Muslim mystics (Zaehner, *Mysticism*, p.92) – we do well to pay heed to H. D. Lewis's sober words: 'We are not meant to be God... but we have every solace in knowing the love of God for us and our abiding destiny in our abiding relation to Him... Christianity has in this way the Jesus of History at the centre of it. It is a position He is never to vacate. This is the radical difference between Christianity and other religions which have much in common with it' (Lewis and Slater, pp.190, 196). Paul sums up the experience to which Christians testify when he says: 'I have been crucified with Christ; it is no longer I who live, but Christ who lives in me; and the life I now live in the flesh I live by faith in the Son of God, who loved me and gave himself for me' (Gal. 2:20); or, again, when he prays for the Ephesians that Christ may dwell in their hearts by faith, and that they may be 'strong to grasp, with all God's people, what is the breadth and length and height and depth of the love of Christ, and to know it, though it is beyond knowledge' (Eph. 3:17ff., NEB). This is what Jesus meant when he spoke of the mutual abiding of him himself (and, indeed, of

Introduction

God the Father) and his disciples. As Visser 't Hooft puts it: 'A Christianity which should think of itself as one of many diverse contributions to the religious life of mankind is a Christianity that has lost its foundation in the New Testament' (Hooft, p.117). For it is of the very essence of New Testament Christianity that it goes back, again and again and again, to God's self-disclosure in the man Christ Jesus, to the atonement he made on the cross, and to the fact of the resurrection. To attempt to enter, ever more deeply, into the meaning of this historic revelation, and the present experience of the living Christ, is central to the Christian life. To try to go beyond it is false and misleading (*cf.* 2 Jn. 9).

2

A unique proclamation?

Introductory

We shall take as our starting-point in our study of 'Christianity and World Religions' the *kerygma*, or proclamation, of the apostolic church, for about this there can be no uncertainty whatever. It is unmistakably clear from the New Testament that Jesus of Nazareth was proclaimed by the apostles as Lord and Saviour, and that the very basis of the apostolic message was his death and resurrection. The one who brought the divine word had himself been declared Son of God, maker and judge of men; for in the *kerygma* (as we find it in the Epistles, the Acts and the Revelation) the messenger has become the message, and his death, resurrection and second advent have become the essence of the proclamation.[1] Thus the heart of the apostolic teaching was that in Jesus God had intervened in human history in a way which was both sufficient and final, for Christ had died 'once for all' (*cf*. Heb. 9:28; 10:10) for our sins, had been buried, and on the third day had been raised to life (1 Cor. 15:3f.).

It is these unique events narrated in the Gospels which, as H. D. Lewis reminds us, form the core of the Christian faith. And he insists that they 'are not to be taken as mere symbols of something beyond them, whether in depths of our own experience or in the absolute being of God. They

---

[1] *Cf*. Günther Bornkamm, 'The Significance of the Historical Jesus for Faith', pp.81, 70.

are not just pictures, but supreme religious reality. The Christian faith, as a distinctive faith, cannot survive the surrender of particularity. It stands or falls with the insistence that it was God himself, in the form of a man[2], who trod this earth two thousand years ago, and died between thieves on a cross' (Lewis and Slater, p.195).

Both the deity of Jesus and the efficacy of his atoning death were, moreover, proved for the apostles by the fact of his resurrection. From the first the confident assertion that Jesus had been raised from death was the basis and starting-point of their proclamation. Nothing else can explain the spontaneous joy of the primitive church, the dramatic transformation of the apostolic band from an attitude of wistful disillusionment and cringing cowardice into that of men whom no persecution could silence, or the triumphant faith of their witness to a crucified felon as the risen Lord of life.[3] As Bornkamm puts it, 'they saw Jesus not as a mere figure of the past who found his tragic end on the cross but as the living Lord, present through the power of his resurrection'; and they proclaimed him as 'the decisive, redemptive, ultimate act of God for the world... All titles of sovereignty which faith now assigns to him express this fact: in him the turning-point of the ages has arrived, the inauguration of salvation, and the nearness and presence of God' (Bornkamm, pp.75, 82).

But the point I want to stress is this: the apostles made this proclamation not as a beautiful story,[4] but as something which actually happened. The uniqueness of the Christian faith consists in the fact that it was founded on a *unique historical event*. It is true that 'empirical Christianity', like all other institutional religions, inevitably includes much that is false and defective as well as a great deal that is noble and true. But it is distinguished from other religions by the event which gave it birth; and it is itself continually corrected and purified in so far as Christians habitually go back to that event – and its necessary implications – as their

---

[2] That is, as 'God-in-manhood', God truly 'made man'.

[3] Although we must, of course, add that it was only after Pentecost, and their inner experience of the promised Spirit, that their transformation was complete.

[4] *Pace* Bultmann and others. But I have discussed the evidence against Bultmann's view, and the way in which some of his disciples are themselves having second thoughts on this, in *Christianity: the Witness of History*.

starting-point, their touchstone and their inspiration.

This, then, will form the central theme of our present study: namely, the way in which this unique historical event distinguishes the Christian faith from all other religions. But this invites two obvious points of challenge: first, the historicity of this alleged event can be – and often has been – called in question; secondly, discussion must inevitably centre on how far it is really unique in its character and content. In terms of world religions the first of these points of challenge must emphasize the gulf between Christianity and those religions in which no real importance is given to historicity, while the second must focus on the essential differences between Christianity and even those religions which do claim a historical foundation – and, indeed, between Christianity and all other religions whatever.

The criterion of history v. mythology

First, then, the question of historicity; for there is all the difference in the world, as Lesslie Newbigin insists, 'between a statement about the nature of God, and a report that God has, at a certain time and place, acted in a certain way. In the latter case the occurrence is the essence of the message. The care which is taken in the New Testament to place the events recorded in the continuum of secular history is in striking contrast to the indifference which is generally shown with regard to the historicity of the events which Hindu piety loves to remember in connection with the character of the gods. There is no serious attempt to relate them to events in secular history, nor is it felt that there would be any advantage to be gained from trying to do so – even if it could be done. Their value is that they illustrate truths about God which would remain true if these particular events had not happened' (*The Finality of Christ*, pp.52ff.).

This is not the place to discuss the vexed question of the vital connection between the Christ of the *kerygma* and the Jesus of history. It is true that liberal scholars have for years made the most strenuous attempts to get behind the apostolic proclamation of a Saviour who was God-in-manhood (truly God, made genuinely man) to an exclusively human Jesus who summoned men to the kingdom of God, who gave ethical teaching epitomized in the Sermon on the Mount, and who suffered the fate which threatens all those who fearlessly proclaim a message which their age and generation is not ready, or willing, to receive. But they soon found that this was a hopeless task, for it is impossible to eliminate all the claims, disputes and miracles from the Gospel records without reducing them to a meaningless distortion, centred on a figure whom no-one would wish to crucify.

So, more recently, the pendulum has swung the other way – from the quest of the Jesus of history to an almost exclusive emphasis on the 'Christ of faith'. The Gospels, we are told (and this is patently true), do not provide the data for a detailed biography of Jesus, and make no attempt to give one. They were documents of faith, written no doubt with a theological intention which largely governed the writers' selection of the teaching and events which they record. But to recognize this is a very different thing from asserting that there is an unbridgeable gulf between the Christ of faith and the Jesus of history. It should, I think, be clear to the most casual reader that the Gospels profess to give us an account of the teaching which Jesus of Nazareth actually gave, the conflict with the religious leaders in which he was continually involved, the miracles which he in fact performed (and which so often constituted the starting-point of his teaching, or the *raison d'être* of official opposition), the way in which he was hounded – and voluntarily surrendered – to a criminal's death, and the triumphant sequel of an empty tomb and a risen Saviour. Even radical criticism, moreover, seems to substantiate most of the essential features of this picture beyond any reasonable doubt, as I have argued elsewhere.[5]

But it is not the details of the Gospel records with which we are primarily concerned in this context. So it will suffice here briefly to discuss, as evidence of the unique historical event which gave birth to the Christian faith, the summary of the apostolic tradition to which passing reference has

[5] See my book *Christianity: the Witness of History. Cf.* also Ferdinand Hahn, p.45.

already been made. In a letter which is indubitably Pauline, and which can be dated with virtual certainty no more than some twenty-five years after the crucifixion, the apostle states that he had already given to his readers by word of mouth (that is, *c*. AD 50) the tradition he was now committing to paper, and which he himself received as an authoritative tradition – initially, in all probability, at the time of his conversion between AD 32 and 35, and in full detail, beyond any question, on his first visit to Jerusalem just three years later, about which he tells us in the first chapter of Galatians. So this takes the tradition right back to within some five years of the event. (*Cf*. Pannenberg, p.90; Dodd, p.168.)

The tradition was this: that 'Christ died for our sins in accordance with the scriptures, that he was buried, that he was raised on the third day in accordance with the scriptures' (1 Cor. 15:3f.). This, Paul tells us,[6] was in no sense distinctively *his* message, but that of all the apostles; and he proceeds to substantiate it by a list of some of the principal witnesses to the resurrection – including the testimony of over five hundred persons who, he asserts quite gratuitously, all saw the risen Christ on one and the same occasion and the majority of whom were still alive (to confirm or deny his statement) when he wrote.

Now it is perfectly true that some theologians are prepared to dispense with this unique event, despite the fact that it represents not only the central thesis in the New Testament but the very foundation of Christian faith down the centuries. Paul Tillich, for example, has committed himself to the statement that 'Religion cannot come to an end, and a particular religion will be lasting to the degree in which it negates itself as a religion. Thus Christianity will be a bearer of the religious answer as long as it breaks through its own particularity' (Tillich, pp.96f.). On this H. D. Lewis – himself no fundamentalist – robustly comments:

This is extremely wide of the mark. We do not begin to do justice to the Christian religion if we make the par-

---

[6] 1 Cor. 15:11. *Pace* S. G. F. Brandon, *Man and his Destiny in the Great Religions*, pp.195ff., who seems to ignore this verse completely.

ticular dispensable in the way implied in this passage . . .
If a Christian does surrender the particular, in the way
commended by Paul Tillich, he should announce himself
boldly as a unitarian. If, as in the case of Tillich, it is not
clear that he has faith in a personal God, he should make
his home among the adherents of other faiths. Indeed,
the proper place for Tillich and many of his followers
today is in the Hindu religion. It is perfectly proper in
that religion to teach that there is a point at which every
religion 'breaks through its particularity', that all our
views are partial expressions of what altogether transcends them. But this is not a consistent course for a
Christian. He can fully allow that there is much that is
hidden from him . . . But at no stage does he hope to pass
beyond the point where his experience derives its
character increasingly from his realization of what God
has done for him in Christ. Nor is there a divorce of the
Jesus of history from the Christ of faith. The crucifixion
did not mean, as some maintain, the total surrender of
the Jesus of history to the Christ of faith. It was God
suffering death in the form of a man, and this remains,
for the Christian, the centre for ever of his life and hope
(Lewis and Slater, pp. 195f.).[7]

The mystery religions

We shall have to return to Hinduism again and again, but it
is appropriate at this point, I think, to turn to those mystery
religions with which Christianity has so often been compared. They were current in the very time and milieu in
which the Christian faith itself had its origin; and it has
often been suggested that it was from the belief, that some
of them included, in a god who died and rose again that the
early Christians postulated the unique event which constitutes the essence of the apostolic proclamation.

That there *are* parallels between the Mysteries and Christianity has been observed, as Bruce M. Metzger tells us,
'since the early centuries of the Church, when both Christian and non-Christian alike commented upon certain

[7] *Cf.* in this context Don Cupitt, who describes himself as 'a Christian Buddhist'.

similarities' (Metzger, p.6). But he goes on to say that a number of the supposed parallels result from an arbitrary amalgamation of heterogeneous elements drawn from a number of different religions, and he quotes Schweitzer's statement that 'Almost all the popular writings fall into this kind of inaccuracy. They manufacture out of the various fragments of information a kind of universal Mystery-religion which never actually existed, least of all in Paul's day'.[8] He also quotes Edwyn R. Bevan's caustic comment: 'Of course if one writes an imaginary description of the Orphic mysteries, as Loisy, for instance, does, filling in the large gaps in the picture left by our data from the Christian eucharist, one produces something very impressive. On this plan, you first put in the Christian elements, and then are staggered to find them there' (Bevan, p.105). So the student of world religions must be on continual guard against what has been called 'parallels made plausible by selective description'.

Nor is it only the critic who may insert Christian elements in some of the mystery religions. In point of fact it is far more likely that Christianity influenced the Mysteries than that they influenced Christianity. As Metzger again observes: 'In what T. R. Glover aptly called "the conflict of religions in the Early Roman Empire", it was to be expected that the hierophants of cults which were beginning to lose devotees to the growing Church should take steps to stem the tide' (Metzger, p.11) On the other hand it is too often overlooked that the New Testament was written almost exclusively by Palestinian Jews, whose 'strict monotheism and traditional intolerance of syncretism' would have militated strongly against any wholesale borrowing from pagan cults. S. H. Hooke emphasizes the 'immunity of the Jew to the influences of the Mystery-cults' and insists that 'between the eternal, immortal, invisible, and only wise God, and the dying and rising gods of the Mystery-cults, there was a great gulf fixed'. So he considers it deeply significant 'that the first Christian community was wholly Jewish, and that the first great original Christian thinker was a Jew' (Hooke, pp.237ff.).

But the basic difference between Christianity and the

[8] Quoted by Metzger, p.9, from A. Schweitzer, *Paul and his Interpreters*, pp.192f.

Mysteries is the historical basis of the one and the mythological character of the others. The deities of the Mysteries were no more than 'nebulous figures of an imaginary past', while the Christ whom the apostolic *kerygma* proclaimed had lived and died only a very few years before the first New Testament documents were written. Even when the apostle Paul wrote his first letter to the Corinthians the majority of some five hundred witnesses to the resurrection were still alive, as we have already seen; and there must have been far more than this who could still testify from their personal experience to his teaching, his personality and his healing touch.

As for the motif of a dying and rising saviour-god, which has so often been compared with the unique event which gave birth to Christianity, Metzger points out that the formal resemblance between them must not be allowed to obscure the great difference in content. In all the Mysteries which tell of a dying god, he dies 'by compulsion and not by choice, sometimes in bitterness and despair, never in a self-giving love'. There is a positive gulf between this and the Christ who asserted that no man could take his life from him, but that he laid it down of his own will (*cf.* Jn. 10:17f.; Mt. 26:53f.); the Johannine picture of the cross as the place where Jesus was 'glorified'; and the Christian celebration of the Passion as a victory over Satan, sin and death. Similarly, there is all the difference in the world between the rising or re-birth of a deity which symbolizes the coming of spring (and the re-awakening of nature) and the resurrection 'on the third day' of a historical person.

It is true that there are certain parallels to this interval between the crucifixion and the empty tomb, for the devotees of Attis commemorated his death on March 22 and his coming to life four days later; there is one account of the death of Osiris, Metzger tells us, which makes the finding and re-animation of his body two or three days after his death; and it has been suggested that Adonis, too, *may* have been depicted as returning to life three days after his demise. But it is significant that the evidence for the commemoration of the *Hilaria*, or the coming of Attis back to life, cannot be traced back beyond the latter part of the second century AD; and the resurrection of Christ on the third day can, as we have seen, be documented as part of the authoritative tradition of the apostolic church from well before the middle of the *first* century. As for Osiris, Metzger writes that 'after his consort Isis had sought and re-assembled thirteen of the fourteen pieces into which his body had been dismembered by his wicked brother..., through the help of magic she was enabled to re-animate' his corpse' (Metzger, pp.19f.). The contrast between this and the testimony of the apostolic church to the resurrection of Jesus is striking. In the case of Adonis, again, the only four witnesses that refer to his resurrection date from the second to the fourth century of the Christian era (Metzger, p.21); so, if borrowing there was by one religion from another, it seems clear which way it went. There is no evidence whatever, that I know of, that the mystery religions had any influence in Palestine in the early decades of the first century. And the difference between the mythological experiences of these nebulous figures and the crucifixion 'under Pontius Pilate' of one of whom eyewitnesses bore testimony to both his death and resurrection is again obvious.

C. S. Lewis's approach

C. S. Lewis has given a good deal of thought to this question (*Miracles*, pp.135ff.) and has suggested an explanation of both the similarities and the differences between Christianity and the Mysteries (or nature religions). I am tempted to outline his argument in his own words, but this would involve too long a quotation.

In the Christian story, he says, God comes right down from the 'heights of absolute being' into time and space; down to humanity, down to the very foundations of the Nature he had himself created. But he 'goes down to come up again and bring the whole ruined world up with him'. In this descent and re-ascent 'everyone will recognise a familiar pattern: a thing written all over the world' – in vegetable life, in animal generation, even in our moral and emotional life. 'Death and re-birth – go down to go up' – this seems to be a basic principle.

This principle is supremely illustrated in the incarnation.

But Lewis argues that the pattern can be found in nature precisely because it was first there in God. It is true that 'the very congruity of this doctrine with all our deepest insights into life and nature may itself make us pause'. Does it not seem to 'fit' so aptly that the suspicion may arise that the idea of the incarnation must have arisen from men seeing this pattern elsewhere, particularly in the annual death of vegetation? 'For there have, of course, been many religions in which the annual drama (so important for the life of the tribe) was almost admittedly the central theme, and the deity – Adonis, Osiris, or another – almost undisguisedly a personification of the corn, a "corn-king" who died and rose again each year. Is not Christ simply another corn-king?'

Now this, he remarks, brings us to a fact which seems, at first sight, very strange indeed. For there *is*, from one point of view, something similar between Christ and Adonis and Osiris – apart from the basic fact that they 'lived nobody knows where or when, while He was executed by a Roman magistrate we know in a year which can be roughly dated'. But the puzzle is this: if Christianity is a religion of that kind, then why is the whole idea so foreign to the New Testament? Corn-religions were both popular and respectable; so why should the analogy be deliberately concealed? If the answer is because the first Christians were Jews, then this raises yet another puzzle, and we must ask ourselves why 'the only religion of a "dying God" which has actually survived and risen to unexampled spiritual heights' sprang from such an alien soil?

'The records, in fact, show us a Person', Lewis insists, 'who *enacts* the part of the Dying God, but whose thoughts and words remain quite outside the circle of religious ideas to which the Dying God belongs. The very thing which the Nature-religions are all about seems to have really happened once: but it happened in a circle where no trace of Nature-religion was present.'

It is at this point that Lewis suggests a solution. He emphasizes that the God who 'came down', died and rose again in Christ was none other than the God of the Old Testament – a God who was, indeed, the glad Creator of wheat, wine and oil, the God of all Nature – 'her inventor, maker, owner and controller' – who constantly works in nature the annual miracle of death and resurrection. And yet he is very different from a nature god, for he himself undergoes no change whatever. Once, and once only in history, he intervened dramatically and decisively in the world of men in the life, death and resurrection of Jesus of Nazareth. So, instead of this decisive act being suggested to the imagination of Christians by the facts of nature, the reality is precisely the other way round: namely, that the annual death and resurrection in-wrought in nature by her Creator provide us with a dim and partial picture of that incarnation, death and resurrection which represent the focal point of the action of the same God in human history, which must have been in his mind from the beginning of creation, and in which alone man can find the ultimate answer to the meaning and destiny of human life – and even of nature itself.

But whatever view is taken of this argument, E. O. James insists that 'there is no valid comparison between the Synoptic story of Jesus of Nazareth and the mythological accounts of the mystery divinities of Eleusis, Thrace, Phrygia or Egypt... Similarly, the belief in the Resurrection of Christ is poles removed from the resuscitation of Osiris, Dionysius, or Attis in an annual ritual based on primitive conceptions of mummification, and the renewal of the new life in the spring. The resemblance between the Christian Easter and the Hilaria in the Attis mystery on March 25th is purely superficial, there being no real points of contact in the "cult-legends" of the two systems' (*In the Fulness of Time*, pp.87f.).

Hinduism

We find this same tendency to mythology rather than history in Hinduism. This is the oldest of all living world religions and, to me, the most baffling, for it is made up of so many strata, it includes such a welter of heterogeneous concepts, and it means so many different things to its vast number of devotees. 'Hindu' is simply the Persian for 'Indian'; and as applied to religion the term came into use only from the time of the Muslim invasions of that country, as a way of distinguishing the age-old beliefs of India (whether of the Indus-valley civilization, the indigenous Dravidians, or the immigrant Aryans) from that of the Muslim invaders. It has been aptly remarked that Hinduism is 'more a culture than a creed', for it still covers a plethora of primitive practices and beliefs alongside a number of highly sophisticated systems of philosophical thought. We shall have to return to Hinduism frequently in the course of this study; but we are now concerned only with any parallel to – or contrast with – the unique historical event which constitutes the very foundation and essence of the Christian faith.

Here the position is clear enough. 'It is no accident', Stephen Neill remarks, 'that there is no indigenous tradition of history-writing in India. The Greeks, the Hebrews and the Muslims all had their understanding of history, and the sense that it was worth while to take trouble to record it. In India the whole genius of the people seems to have been turned inwards to contemplation and the development of speculative thought... Traditionally the Hindu does not attach great importance to the events that occur in the three-dimensional world of space and time, or to the human beings that take part in them... Thus the Hindu has in the past been inclined to take pride in the fact that Hinduism is a religion of pure ideas, and in this respect to contrast Christianity unfavourably with it as a religion that is dependent on history' (Neill, pp.87ff.). Lesslie Newbigin tells us that he has never forgotten the astonishment with which a devout and learned teacher of the Rāmakrishna Mission regarded him when he discovered that the bishop was prepared to rest his whole faith as a Christian upon 'the substantial historical truth of the record concerning Jesus in the New Testament'. To the Hindu it 'seemed axiomatic that such vital matters of religious truth could not be allowed to depend upon the accidents of history. If the truths which Jesus exemplified and taught are true, then they are true always and everywhere, whether a person called Jesus ever lived or not' (Newbigin, *The Finality of Christ*, p.50).

But for the Christian the 'truths which Jesus exemplified and taught' cannot be separated from the historical facts. It is not enough to postulate that the nature and character of

God are such as Jesus declared them to be; for it is pre-eminently through what Jesus *was* and *did* that God's nature and character stand revealed; and it is meaningless to speak of the efficacy of his atoning death unless he did in fact die. But it is true that, with the event, we also need the interpretation put on that event by the apostles.

No doubt God reveals himself continually, in one way or another, at all times and in all places – had we only the eyes to see. This is a question with which we must grapple later. But this does not mean that there must have been successive incarnations, and that all that was lacking was men like the apostles to apprehend and interpret them. On the contrary, the Christian faith, based on the apostolic testimony, is that God acted in Jesus in a way which was unique, which was never to be repeated, and which constitutes the decisive point in human history.[9]

There are, therefore, a number of fundamental differences between the Christian doctrine of the incarnation and the Hindu belief in the ways in which the 'Ultimate Reality' or one of the gods has made himself known to men. First, the *avatārs*, or 'descents', in which many Hindus believe – and which awaken in some of them, beyond question, a passionate devotion – for the most part[1] concern mythological rather than historical figures. A Hindu may, indeed, commit himself to an *avatār* without any conviction that such a being ever existed in history.[2] Secondly, those Hindus who believe in a personal God (whether Vishnu, Śiva or Kālī, the mother goddess) conceive of Vishnu as having 'descended' in a whole sequence of *avatārs*[3] – sometimes in the form of a fish, sometimes that of an animal, but usually that of a man. Many of these (Krishna, Rāma, *etc.*) are themselves worshipped as gods – to all intents and purposes – in popular Hinduism (as also are Vishnu, Śiva and Kālī, of course); but they are all regarded by more sophisticated persons as different mani-

---

[9] *Cf.* Newbigin, *op. cit.*, p.76. *Cf.* also N. Smart, *World Religions: a Dialogue*, pp.90ff.

[1] An exception to this may be found in those who accept Sri Rāmakrishna, a mystic reformer born in 1836, or Chaitanya, a revivalist worshipper of Vishnu born in 1845, as *avatārs*. Others would add the Buddha.

[2] *Cf.* Allen, p.108. But, again, there can be no doubt that the simple Hindu takes these *avatārs* literally.

[3] Many Hindus postulate that there will be ten in all, of which the tenth is still to come. Many, again, include the Buddha among them.

festations of the Supreme Being. It is quite easy for a Hindu, therefore, to accept Christ as yet another incarnation of the deity – but, as Gandhi put it, not to give him a solitary or supreme throne.

Thirdly, to the philosophical Hindu a belief in these incarnations represents a somewhat low level of spiritual perception; but he will concede that one who cannot 'apprehend the deity in itself, even in a personal form, may need the help of some human figure to which he may cling as the only means by which . . . the divine can penetrate his spirit'.[4] Fourthly, some of these incarnations of the deity are depicted as falling very far short of what we should regard as moral perfection. And fifthly, some of the leading schools of Hindu thought are purely monistic. To the Advaita Vedānta, for example, there is only one Ultimate Reality, the neuter Brahman, which is true and real. All else – physical, human, or so-called 'divine' – is mere 'illusion' or 'appearance' (*māyā*), with no abiding significance.

It seems unnecessary, therefore, to labour the contrast between these *avatārs* and the incarnation as Christians know it. Suffice it to say that it has always been emphasized that this was a historical event; that it was once for all, unrepeatable and 'without parallel or substitute' (*cf.* Rom. 6:10; Heb. 10:10); and that it concerned the one who was not only the 'Father's only Son' but was also morally perfect, 'full of grace and truth' (*cf.* Jn. 1:14). This finds a very early expression in the words of Paul in his first letter to the Corinthians: 'We know that an idol is nothing at all in the world and that there is no God but one. For even if there are so-called gods, whether in heaven or on earth (as indeed there are many "gods" and many "lords"), yet for us there is but one God, the Father, from whom all things came and for whom we live; and there is but one Lord, Jesus Christ, through whom all things came and through whom we live' (1 Cor. 8:4–6). In these three verses Paul is, I think, making three distinct points: first, that the so-called gods of other religions have no real existence, and that an idol, as such, is 'nothing'; secondly, that there are, none the less – behind and beside these false gods – demons and other supernatural

---

[4] *Cf.* Neill, p.83, summarizing the views of the late President Radhakrishnan. But others take quite a different view (see. pp.93f., 102, below).

beings sometimes called 'gods' or 'lords' even in the Bible, but they are in fact created beings; and thirdly, that there is only one true God, our Father, *by* whom all were created, and one Lord, Jesus Christ, *through* whom (as the eternal Word of God) all were created – and that we live for God because of the redemption that is in and through Christ.

Shintōism and tribal religions

Shintōism, the Way of the Gods, is the national religion of Japan. It has no systematic doctrine and no philosophy of its own, and seems to combine features of primitive nature worship with Emperor worship, while its moral teaching owes much today to Confucianism and still more to Buddhism. Sometimes the objects of veneration are mountains, islands, trees, rocks or waterfalls, which may or may not be connected with some legendary story or belief. Sometimes, again, the object of veneration is an animal-god or plant, or some mythological god or goddess. But none of this has any clear basis in history – except, of course, the different Emperors of Japan. Much the same can be said of those primal religions, all the world over, which were formerly often subsumed under the title of Animism – of which primitive Shintōism was, indeed, the variety characteristic of Japan. 'Animism' basically consists in the worship of, and endeavour to propitiate, those spirits which are believed to reside in natural objects such as trees, rocks or springs; but this is commonly combined with the veneration of the dead (who are regarded, together with the living and those still unborn, as constituting the mystical entity of the tribe or family), and sometimes with fetishism, totemism, taboos and magical practices of various sorts. But with Animism we virtually come back to those beliefs in a 'corn-king' and other features of nature religions which we have discussed already. Neither in Shintōism nor in other primal religions is there anything remotely comparable, therefore, with the unique historical event which was both the origin and the substance of the *kerygma* of the apostolic church.

Religions with a historical basis

Zoroastrianism

With Zoroastrianism we come to those religions whose founders were certainly historical figures, although there is considerable doubt about the date when Zarathushtra (Zoroaster) actually lived and prophesied. Some scholars today opt for a very early date (*c.* 1500 BC) and claim that he was 'the first of the great prophets of the world's religions' (*cf.* J. R. Hinnells, in *The World's Religions*, p.80). It has for a long time been more usual, however, to accept the dating traditionally preserved by the Zoroastrians themselves, which would place the beginning of his ministry about 588 BC (*cf.* R. C. Zaehner, in *Living Faiths*, p.200). In this case he would have been a near contemporary of Lao-tzu (the founder of Taoism) and of Confucius in China, of Gautama the Buddha and Mahāvīra (the founder of Jainism) in India, and of Jeremiah and Ezekiel in Israel. Thus the possibility of cross-fertilization is obvious.

Zoroastrianism has almost vanished as a living religion, and survives only among the small (but influential) Parsee community and a few thousand of the 'faithful' in Iran. For many years, however, it was the official religion of the then mighty Persian empire. Its importance today lies chiefly in the influence it has had on other religions and in the fact that, in one of the forms in which it has developed, it is almost completely dualist in its teaching. Thus almost all life's vicissitudes can be explained largely in terms of which deity or power – the good or the evil – was in control at the relevant time!

The holy book of Zoroastrianism is the *Avesta*, only a fraction of which still survives, and only part of which (a series of *Gāthās*, or hymns, written in the first person) can with confidence be ascribed to Zoroaster in person. It seems clear that he was himself a monotheist who claimed to hold converse with a God who was wholly good (Ahura Mazdāh, the 'Wise Lord'); and he did much to combat the primitive polytheism of his 'Indo-Iranian' forebears. In his belief, Ahura Mazdāh was in no way responsible for the evil in the world. This was the work of the Lie (*druj*), named at that time Angra-Mainyu. Zoroaster did not accept any doctrine of 'original sin', and believed that man was completely free to choose whether he would follow the wise 'Creator' (later known as Ohrmazd) or the evil 'Destroyer' (later called the accursed Ahrimān).

I must not get involved, in this context, with the inter-relation of these two forces or the way in which Zoroastrian thought and teaching developed. Our sole concern here is with Zoroaster's 'proclamation', which seems to have consisted in an unequivocal summons to men and women to exercise their free, unbiased freedom to follow Truth and Righteousness and to fight against the Lie and his followers. Their ultimate judgment would be according to the choice they had made.

Confucianism, Taoism and Buddhism

In Confucianism and Taoism we find religions which might almost equally well be described as philosophies. This is particularly true of Confucianism, with its strong emphasis on ethics; but in Taoism an abstruse philosophy is strangely blended with a riot of cosmology, magic and even demonology. There is, indeed, some doubt about the date which should be assigned to Lao-tzu, and it has even been questioned whether he was in fact a historical figure. However this may be, he came to be venerated as one who had been carried in his mother's womb for some seventy or eighty years, and had then (not altogether surprisingly!) been mature at birth.

In Buddhism the outstanding 'historical event' is undoubtedly the vivid conviction of the transience of all things, and the mystery of suffering, which impelled Gautama to forsake the luxurious life of a young Kshatriya prince, and even his sleeping wife and infant son, first for the traditional discipline of the ascetic life and then for solitary meditation – followed, in due course, by his 'Enlightenment'. Far from keeping his new-found know-ledge to himself, moreover, he set out on a wandering minis-try to teach others how they, too, could escape from the bondage of desire and attain to a state of passionless peace.

But Buddhism, like the Hinduism from which it sprang, has developed in a plethora of different forms. In the

Theravāda form ('the doctrine of the elders' – which still prevails, to a greater or lesser degree, in Sri Lanka, Burma, Thailand, Kampuchea and Laos) the Buddha is not in any sense a god, or even a mediator, saviour or redeemer, but the supreme teacher and example. He points the way, but Theravādins insist that man can expect no outside help in regard to the *karma* (of merit or demerit) which each individual accumulates for himself throughout his present and past lives. But in course of time a very different form of Buddhism, known as Mahāyāna (the 'great vehicle' – in contrast to the term Hīnayāna, or 'lesser vehicle', by which they commonly referred to the Theravādins), spread – in a variety of different sects – in Nepal, Sikkim, Bhutan, Tibet, China, Mongolia, Vietnam, Korea and Japan. In Mahāyāna Buddhism – to quote Charles Davis's exceedingly concise summary of a variety of very different sects and doctrines –

> the historical Buddha receded into the background. A religion of worship developed, directed to heavenly Buddhas, notably Amitabha, and to various great Bodhisattvas.[5] These Buddhas and Bodhisattvas became saviours, who prepared a Pure Land[6] or paradise for their faithful, where conditions were more favourable for the attainment of Nirvāna.[7] Hope of reception into the Pure Land of Amitabha took the place for some of Nirvāna as a goal. The means of salvation [for them] was now the invocation of the heavenly Buddha in faith (*Christ and the World Religions*, p.106).

Yet another variety of Buddhism, which is fairly well known in the West today, is Zen Buddhism. This evolved in China in the thirteenth century from the Ch'an school, and became widespread in Japan. Fundamentally it is much closer, in most respects, to Theravāda than Mahāyāna doctrine, but differs sharply from the former in positing an enlightenment not only at the end of the Path, but here and

[5] Beings of Enlightenment who defer their own deliverance from this world in order to save others.

[6] Pure Land Buddhism is widespread today in Japan and was so, previously at least, in China.

[7] The passionless peace, to which reference has already been made.

now as its followers persevere in the Path itself. To attain this Zen-Buddhists must meticulously follow a special system of posture, breathing and meditation, very similar to the Hindu Yoga regime.

It is clear, then, that in Zoroastrianism, Confucianism, Taoism and Buddhism there is either a system of ethical and religious teaching in which man is virtually left to work out his own salvation, or else (in various sects) a promise of supernatural help through some largely mythological saviour. So the contrast between their teaching and that of the apostolic proclamation of forgiveness, new life and eternal salvation through a historical person (to whose life, atoning death, resurrection and ascension they could actually testify) is obvious. Thus in Buddhism, as H. D. Lewis asserts,

> The peculiar significance ascribed by Christians to certain historical events has no place ... and Buddha himself, according to the famous text which described his decease, disavowed at the time of his death any peculiar claims to be made on his behalf as the instrument of salvation. It was the doctrine that he bequeathed to others and it was the doctrine that really mattered, although this advice was extensively disregarded ... There is certainly no once for all redeeming event whose significance is to be preserved at all cost (Lewis and Slater, pp.155f., 173).

Islam

In Islam we come to a religion which is not only clearly historical but also rigidly monotheistic. We shall have to consider its teachings about salvation and revelation in subsequent chapters; but the relevant point in the present context is that to the Muslim the one unforgivable sin is that of *shirk*, or associating anyone or anything with the Almighty. The very idea of an incarnation of the deity is therefore anathema, or simple blasphemy, particularly to the orthodox or Sunnī Muslim (and the Sunnīs represent about ninety per cent of some 700 million or so contemporary Muslims). To them Muhammad was God's inspired prophet, and they have come to regard him as impeccable and infallible, but not in any sense divine. It is partly for this reason that they commonly object to being called 'Muhammadans', since they think this term implies that they regard Muhammad in much the same way as Christians regard Christ. To the Muslim it is the divine revelation of which Muhammad was the mouthpiece, rather than any historical event, which is all important.

But as in so many religions, it was not long before differences of opinion and multiplication of sects began to appear in Islam too. It was during the first century of the Muslim era that the Shī'a[8], or 'sect' of 'Alī, broke away – – in some sense, at least – from the main body of orthodox Islam. In due course the Shī'a itself split up into a number of conflicting sects; but they were all united in the belief that God could not have left the leadership of the Muslim community to the vagaries of human election, but must himself have designated a leader and have given him – whether directly or through Muhammad – esoteric teaching about the principles of the faith. And who, other than 'Alī (a cousin and son-in-law of Muhammad, a doughty warrior and an eloquent orator), should this be?

The Shī'ī sects were also united in their belief that when 'Alī died he must have been succeeded by another Imām, or leader, who could continue to give authoritative teaching to the community. The splits between them were, in fact, almost all concerned with disputes about the succession to the Imamate. Most of them agreed that this was confined to the Prophet's grandchildren through 'Alī and Fātima, Muhammad's only surviving child. Usually, moreover, the succession went from father to eldest son – and all the Shī'īs except the Zaydīs came to believe that the Imāms, like Muhammad himself, were impeccable and infallible, and that a 'divine light-substance' which had been inherent in Muhammad and earlier prophets passed from one Imām to his successor by a special form of metempsychosis.

The largest Shī'ī sub-sect – the Twelvers (or Ithnā

[8] Arabists may find some difficulty in distinguishing the 'ayn from the hamza in transliterated Arabic words, because the wedges used as opening and closing quotation marks are so similar in this type-face. But there *is* a slight difference, which I hope can be discerned. The dots commonly printed below certain consonants in transliterated Arabic, and either above or below them in Sanskrit, have been omitted to save expense.

'Asharīya) – believe that the twelfth of these Imāms withdrew, in 260 AH, and went into hiding 'in the will of God'. In their belief he is, indeed, still alive, the sole medium of spiritual blessing; and he will one day reappear to bring in the golden age. In the meantime it is only the leading religious figures (the *mujtahids*) who can in any sense claim to represent him. So it is relevant to remember that the present 'Islamic Revolution' in Iran is very largely confined to the Iranian members of this comparatively small sub-sect (predominant though it is in that country); that it is on a distinctly idiosyncratic view of their teaching that al-Khomaini has secured the final voice, in their current constitution, for the foremost religious lawyer (*al-Faqīh*); that it is on the strength of his inflexible opposition to the Shah (and consequent political leadership) rather than his pre-eminence in legal learning that he himself now holds this position; that the 'Revolutionary Courts' in Iran have been dispensing a form of 'justice' which is essentially revolutionary rather than Islamic; and that thousands of their real or alleged opponents have been executed for 'fighting against God' or 'causing corruption in the earth' – words found in the Qur'ān in regard to what is normally interpreted as the prescribed penalty only for the *hadd* offence of highway robbery in the course of which a murder has been committed.

The Ismā'īlīs, on the other hand, chose a different line of succession after the sixth Imām. At a later date they subdivided once again; and the twenty-first Imām recognized by one section, the Musta'līs, also went into hiding (although, unlike the Imām of the Twelvers, he is not regarded as still supernaturally alive, but as having been followed by an unknown number of successors), while the Imām of the other section, the Nizārīs, is still present in the person of the Agha Khān – and is accorded, at least by the less sophisticated of his followers, almost divine honours. It can, indeed, be said that some of the Shī'īs have come to believe in what is very near to a principle of incarnation.

It is not altogether surprising, then, that further splits from the Shī'a have led to the founding of new religions. Such are the Druze, the Bābīs and the Bahā'īs. The

Druze derive their name from al-Darazī, but their real leader was Hamza, who regarded the Fātimid Caliph al-Hākim as the 'embodiment of the ultimate One' (*Encyclopaedia of Islam*, 'Durūz') and the first cosmic principle. The Bābīs are named after Sayyid 'Alī Muhammad of Shirāz, who was born in 1819 and was recognized as the 'gateway' (*bāb*) to truth, the initiator of a new prophetic cycle and the 'mirror of the breath of God' (*Encyclopaedia of Islam*, 'Bāb'); while the Bahā'īs are those who broke away from other followers of the Bāb in favour of Bahā' Allāh, one of the Bāb's first disciples, who declared himself to be 'He whom God shall Manifest'. As such, he certainly claimed to be a prophet in his own right, but he did not teach any doctrine of incarnation. Each of these three religions now has a theology and ethic of its own.

Bahā'ism represents a syncretic religion which combines elements drawn from several faiths in a novel synthesis. This is also true, in some measure, of the Ahmadīya movement, although this has never wholly broken away from the body of Islam. Its founder, Ghulām Ahmad Khān, born in the Punjab about 1839, not only claimed to be the Mahdī (or 'Rightly-guided One') whom Muslims expect but also the fulfilment of numerous Messianic prophecies in the Old Testament and even an *avatār* of Krishna. One section of his followers regard him as a prophet in his own right, although 'within the revelation of Islam', while a more moderate section has resiled from this claim (which amounts to apostasy in the eyes of orthodox Muslims) and say that he was only a reformer (*mujaddid*).

But however this may be, what is crystal clear is that Islam as a whole makes no claim to any parallel to the unique historical event on which Christianity is founded; on the contrary, it would regard any such claim as blasphemous. To Muslims – even including the Shī'a – the Christian doctrine of the incarnation is *shirk*, for they think that Christians have put a mortal man, albeit a prophet who was virgin-born, on an equality with God. They find it desperately difficult to realize that in fact the movement, in Christianity, is not up but down: not exalting a man and equating him with God, but worshipping a God who became man. They also flatly deny that Jesus was ever crucified.[9] Instead, they believe that when the Jewish leaders came upon him with the intention of crucifying him, God could not allow this to happen to his chosen messenger, mere man though he was; so he caught him up to heaven to deliver him out of their hands, and then – by what we can only, I suppose, regard as a piece of divine deception – cast the likeness of Jesus on someone else, who was crucified by mistake in his place. So the unique historical event which Christians commemorate on Good Friday and Easter Day meets from Muslims an unequivocal denial, in spite of all the evidence to the contrary.

Judaism

Finally, we come to Judaism – another historical and strictly monotheistic religion. Christians, of course, believe that in Judaism God had in fact, down many centuries, been preparing the way – by the call of Abram and the patriarchs, the exodus from Egypt, the covenant and commandments of Sinai, the inspired messages of a long succession of prophets and the visions of certain apocalyptists – for the unique historical event which not only gave rise to their own faith but heralded the world's salvation by the birth, ministry, death and exaltation of Jesus. It was in his person and his 'work' that the promises to the patriarchs, the types and shadows of the Mosaic law, the dimly perceived predictions of the prophets and even the dreams of apocalyptists, had been fulfilled. But Jews themselves usually look back to the exodus as the dominant historical event in their past history.

Then Israel as a whole not only rejected their Messiah when he came, but misunderstood those prophecies that had depicted him as more than an exclusively human and national deliverer, had foretold his sufferings and death, and had accorded that death a saving and redemptive significance. So it was partly in human ignorance, and

[9] Except, that is, for the Ahmadīya, who have adopted Venturini's theory that Jesus was indeed crucified, but did not *die* on the cross. See my book *Christianity: the Witness of History*, pp.62ff.

partly by reason of human sin, that when Jesus 'came to his own home ... his own people received him not' (Jn. 1:11). Instead, practising Jews still look forward to a personal Messiah, or some sort of 'Messianic Age', which is yet to come.[1]

Religious Pluralism and the New Testament

In one sense this brings us back to where we began: the unique apostolic proclamation, which rests four-square on the atoning death and triumphant resurrection of the Jesus of history. But first we must, I think, turn aside once more, as in the previous chapter, to face the challenge of Religious Pluralism in its contention that, while the different religions we have passed in brief review in this chapter each has its quite different 'proclamation', yet at the end of the day they can all be regarded as divergent paths (each with its distinctive strengths and weaknesses) to the same ultimate truth.

This is, of course, no new challenge. But it has been taken up with renewed zest in recent years by a number of writers, each of whom naturally has his individual stance. I think, however, that the general approach can conveniently, and not unfairly, be discussed in terms of the chapter entitled 'Jesus and the World Religions' contributed by John Hick to *The Myth of God Incarnate*. To this reference has already been made; and it can also conveniently be consulted in *God Has Many Names* (where virtually the same chapter is repeated). I have felt tempted to refer to his views several times in connection with one religion or another; but the fact that he himself deals with most of the relevant points in a single chapter (which, with respect, seems to be a somewhat strange amalgam of heterogeneous assertions – some obviously true, some misleading or mutually inconsistent, and some, in my view, totally unacceptable) makes it more convenient to devote a special section to this challenge.

As we have seen, Hick's own views have changed radically in the course of the last few years. But I trust that I

---

[1] For a much more adequate treatment, *cf.* my *God's Law and God's Love*, ch. 2.

shall not be misrepresenting his present position if I rely on statements made in *The Centre of Christianity* (1977) as well as in *God Has Many Names*.

Hick has no doubt that Jesus was a truly historical figure; and, in spite of an occasional aside about 'the largely unknown man of Galilee' – in the course of which he goes so far as to state that 'some have pictured him as a stern law-giver and an implacable judge' (*God Has Many Names*, pp.59f.) – he himself 'sees the Nazarene' as 'a man of God, living in the unseen presence of God, and addressing God as *abba*, father'. His life was, indeed, such a 'continuous response to the divine love' that it 'vibrated, as it were, to the divine life; and as a result his hands could heal the sick, and the "poor in spirit" were kindled to new life in his presence'. If, therefore, 'you or I had met him . . . we would have felt the absolute claim of God confronting us, summoning us to give ourselves wholly to him . . . as his children and as agents of his purposes on earth'; for Jesus was 'so totally conscious of God' that we, too, should have felt that we were in the divine presence. But there would always have been 'the possibility of turning away from this challenging presence'. So 'to encounter Jesus, whether in the flesh or through the New Testament pictures of him, has always been liable to be a turning point in anyone's life, a crisis of salvation or judgment' (pp.64f.).

So far, so good. But how, Hick asks, 'did Jews come, with their Gentile fellow-Christians', actually 'to worship a human being, thus breaking their unitarian monotheism in a way which eventually required the sophisticated metaphysics of the Trinity?' First, he suggests, Jesus was a figure of such 'tremendous spiritual power' that his disciples were 'born again' into an experience, 'transmitted scarcely diminished for several generations', which was 'focused on Jesus as Messiah and Lord'. But 'before long' pressures must have developed for them 'to use titles which would more explicitly present the challenge of Jesus' saving power, first within the Jewish community and then within the Gentile world of the Roman empire. And these could only be the highest titles available.' 'Ideas of divinity embodied in human life' were, he insists, 'widespread in the ancient world, so that there is nothing surprising in the deification of Jesus in that environment.' Why, even within Judaism itself, 'the notion of a man being called son of God already had a long tradition behind it' (*cf.* Ps. 2:7). So Christians eventually made 'the very significant transition from "son of God" to "God the Son", the Second Person of the Trinity'. In other words, they came to give a literal and theological meaning to terms which were originally meta-phorical and poetical (pp.66ff.).

Now of course it is true that 'ideas of divinity [of *some* sort] embodied in human life were widespread in the ancient world' – although it may be questioned how seriously many of them were taken. But is it really credible that Paul the Pharisee, brought up in 'the strictest party of our religion' (Acts 26:5), would have regularly spoken of Jesus as 'the Lord Jesus Christ' and 'the Son of God' (or 'God's own Son'), would have continually coupled his name with that of 'God the Father', and would even, very occasionally, have written of him in terms which, on their most natural interpretation, actually refer to him as 'God' (*cf.* Rom. 9:5; Tit. 2:13) – a phenomenon which recurs in other New Testament passages (*cf.* Jn. 1:1f., 18; 20:28; Heb. 1:8; 2 Pet. 1:1) – had it not been for his own encounter with the ascended Lord, and the testimony of others to his resurrection?[2] Most of the verses just cited *can*, it is true, be translated in a way that avoids this nomenclature; and in John 1:18 and Acts 20:28 alternative readings are available. No-one, of course, suggests that a certain distinction between Jesus and God the Father was not always retained, but their essential unity was emphasized, explicitly and implicitly, time and again.

In any case, it is inescapable that Paul refers to the pre-existence of Christ (although not, of course, of Jesus of Nazareth as such), without any feeling that he needs to explain his terms, in passages such as Philippians 2:6–11 (which very possibly represents the quotation of a pre-Pauline hymn), 1 Corinthians 8:6 (*cf.* 10:4) and Colossians 1:15ff. – and the same phenomenon occurs in Hebrews 1:2 and, repeatedly, in John's Gospel (*cf.* 1:1–4, 30; 6:62; 8:58; and 17:5, 24).

[2] Other passages that may possibly bear this meaning are Col. 2:2; 2 Thes. 1:12; 1 Jn. 5:20; and, according to a variant reading, 1 Tim. 3:16.

Somewhat similar remarks could be made about the term *Kyrios* (Lord). As we have seen, Paul spoke almost in one breath of the 'many lords' in pagan culture in sharp distinction from the Christians' 'one Lord, Jesus Christ' whom he conjoined with the Father as both the source and the goal of life (1 Cor. 8:6). Again, after emphasizing in the Christological hymn in Philippians 2 (to which reference has already been made) that it was because of his death on the cross that God had bestowed on Jesus 'the name which is above every name', Paul boldly transfers to Jesus the great monotheistic passage in Isaiah 45:23 when he adds 'that at the name of Jesus every knee should bow, in heaven and on earth and under the earth, and every tongue confess that Jesus Christ is Lord, to the glory of God the Father' (*cf.* Moule, *The Origin of Christology*, pp.41f.).

In the Gospels, moreover, passages in which Jesus is recorded as simply referring to himself as 'the Son' are by no means confined to John, or to contexts (like Jn. 5:16–40) in which the Jews reacted strongly to what they regarded as blasphemy. He is reported as explicitly referring to himself as 'the Son' – and in close juxtaposition with 'the Father' – in Matthew 11:27 (*cf.* Lk. 10:22) and Mark 13:32, for example, and by implication in certain other passages. But Hick virtually ignores the Synoptists (with the solitary exception of Mark 1:1), numberless Pauline references, the Epistle to the Hebrews and other New Testament evidence when he writes of 'the developing tradition' speaking of Jesus 'in terms which he himself did not use' and understanding him 'by means of a complex of beliefs which was *only gradually formed* by later generations of his followers' (*God Has Many Names*, p.62. My italics), and blandly states that what happened was that 'his Jewish followers hailed him as their Messiah, and this somewhat mysterious title developed in its significance within the mixed Jewish-Gentile church *ultimately* to the point of deification' (p.66. My italics).

Our concern in this chapter is with the apostolic proclamation rather than its implications in regard to salvation or the nature of God. But it seems clear that the evidence in the New Testament about the origins of the Christian faith is very different from Hick's hypothesis. In an indubitably

Pauline Epistle (as we have seen in pp.49f., above) the apostle records the 'tradition' he had himself 'received' (*cf.* 1 Cor. 15:3–7) – a tradition he must have received in its fullness, including the list of some of the principal witnesses, 'within a very few years after Jesus was crucified – almost certainly not more than seven years, possibly no more than four' (Dodd, p.168). 'Something had happened to these men', Dodd continues, 'which they could describe only by saying that they had "seen the Lord". This is not an appeal to any generalized "Christian experience". It refers to a particular series of occurrences, unique in character, unrepeatable, and confined to a limited period' – for Paul seems to make a distinction between his own experience on the Damascus road (which can, indeed, be described as a vision) and the 'appearances' of the risen Lord during the 'forty days'[3] – which, it seems, constituted the united testimony of the apostolic church (1 Cor. 15:11). In other words, the witness to the resurrection clearly goes back to the very genesis of the church and was from the first fundamental to its life, doctrine and proclamation.

This is, indeed, frankly admitted by Hick in *The Centre of Christianity*, where he states that 'but for this mysterious event which dominated and coloured the thinking of the first generation of believers, Christianity would never have been more than a dying memory of a dead prophet. But the early Christian preaching as we hear it echoed in the Acts of the Apostles and the Letters of Paul was never about a dead teacher or healer or prophet or even Messiah. It was always about Jesus, who had been raised by God from the dead'. But then Hick proceeds to waver about how the resurrection should be understood. Although his present theological views necessarily incline him to believe that the resurrection appearances 'consisted in visions (technically hallucinations, perhaps auditory as well as visual)', he gives passing recognition to *some* of the evidence against

---

[3] *Cf.* my *Christianity: the Witness of History*, p.99. 'It is true that in 1 Cor. 15 Paul refers to his own encounter with the risen Christ as though it were on a par with the appearances to the other apostles; but this probably means that his experience was as real and "objective" as theirs, not that theirs was as "visionary" as his.' *Cf.* also J. A. T. Robinson, in *The Interpreter's Dictionary of the Bible*, Vol. 4, p.48. After stating that 'there is little basis' for concluding that 'Paul regarded all the other appearances as conforming to the pattern of his own vision on the Damascus Road', Robinson adds: 'So far from regarding his own vision as normative, he marvels at his right to include it in the series at all.'

this view. In any case, he concludes: 'In the days after Jesus' crucifixion something momentous happened to bring the disciples' faith back to life, and indeed to more than its former life; and according to the account of the Christian community itself that momentous event was the resurrection of Jesus to a life that was mysteriously more than his former life. He was present now in such a way that they could no longer doubt his lordship. And so his resurrection became the foundation of their faith' (pp.24ff.).

But at this point Hick quotes a remark by G. B. Caird: 'Let us suppose that tomorrow you were confronted with irrefutable evidence that an acquaintance whom you had good reason to believe dead had been seen alive by reliable witnesses. You would certainly feel compelled to revise some of your ideas about science, but I doubt whether you would . . . conclude that your acquaintance was divine, or that a stamp of authenticity had been placed on all he ever said or did. . . . .'[4] (*God Has Many Names*, p.64). No, indeed. One's first instinct, I suppose, would be to check up on the evidence that the person concerned had really died; next, to make sure that he was now genuinely alive in the ordinary sense we attribute to that term; and thirdly to think long and deeply about the qualities of the person concerned.

In the case of Jesus, there can be no reasonable doubt that he had really died – unless, of course, one is convinced by Venturini's theory (more recently adopted, with very different permutations, by the Ahmadīya community, Hugh Schonfield and Duncan Derrett[5]). Nor is there any justification for regarding the risen Christ as merely a resuscitated corpse. The evidence points strongly to the fact that he was not a ghost, phantom or disembodied spirit, but had a 'body' which could be recognized and touched, and could even eat; and it seems clear that what Paul, for example, believed was that his crucified body had been transformed in the tomb from a 'natural' or 'animal'

---

[4] Quoted from 'The Christological Basis of Christian Hope', in *The Christian Hope*, p.10.

[5] For comments on this theory, the Ahmadīya and *The Passover Plot*, cf. my *Christianity: the Witness of History*, pp.63ff. And Strauss's objection to any form of this theory ('It is impossible that a being who had stolen half dead out of the sepulchre . . . could have given the disciples the impression that he was the Conqueror over death and the grave, the Prince of life, an impression which lay at the bottom of their future ministry') would be equally applicable to the wildly imaginative 'reconstruction' in Derrett's *The Anastasis*.

body into a 'spiritual body' (*cf.* Pannenberg, pp.75ff.; Caird, *The Gospel of Luke*, pp.255ff.). The 'perishable' and 'mortal' had been raised 'imperishable' and 'immortal' (1 Cor. 15:41ff., 50ff. *Cf.* Rom. 6:9; Phil. 3:21).

But what about the third criterion: 'the qualities of the person concerned'? Hick gives us no inkling that the sentences he quotes from Caird are preceded by the statement: 'I hold that the historical evidence both for the resurrection appearances and for the empty tomb is earlier and more reliable than sceptics, outside or inside of the Church, have been ready to allow. But at one point I agree with the sceptics, that this evidence *by itself* proves very little. Such criticism has commonly been directed against the accounts of the empty tomb. "Let us suppose", wrote Maurice Goguel, "that a document was found which established beyond cavil that on the morning of the third day the tomb of Jesus was found empty. Let us suppose that the demonstrative evidence was accepted by all historians. Do you imagine it would be enough to convert them to the Christian faith?" To this I would add that the same must be said of the resurrection appearances.'

It is immediately after these words that the sentences Hick quotes occur. And all the rest of Caird's paper (pp. 10–24) is devoted to asking – and answering – the question: 'Why then did the first Christians find the evidence of the appearances and the empty tomb so convincing and so full of far-reaching implications?' – a question which refers back to his immediately preceding sentence (quoted by Hick out of context and in a truncated form) which asks, as we have seen, whether one would conclude that 'an acquaintance' whom you had good reason to believe dead, yet had been seen alive by reliable witnesses, 'was divine, or that a stamp of authority had been placed on all he ever said or did, or even that he would not yet, at some time in the future, have to die'.

To this last point I have already referred: Jesus was *not* merely resuscitated, but raised by God to a new form of life, and would never die again. But Caird deals at some length with the answer to the question: 'Why then did they believe?' His initial reply is that 'The answer must lie in their experience of the earthly Jesus; there was something about his earthly life which made the resurrection, *once it had happened*, seem the natural, proper and convincing sequel' (p.11. My italics).[6] But that the 'sequel' *was* so convincing, he claims, 'is the general consensus of the New Testament'. In this context he quotes the words attributed to Peter in Acts 2:24 'God raised him to life again, setting him free from the pangs of death, because it could not be that death should keep him in its grip', and also the reference in Hebrews 7:16 to 'the power of an indestructible life'.

It is in this context that Caird remarks: 'Granted that the speed with which the early Church came to accord divine honours to Jesus of Nazareth is one of the most impressive facts of New Testament theology, it would nevertheless be rash to maintain that belief in the incarnation antedated and provided a warrant for a belief in the resurrection.' The 'warrant' lay, rather, in the fact that Jesus' whole life had been lived in such 'close communion with God', in such utter 'obedience to the demands of love', and in such 'willing participation in the divine purpose of redemption' (p.12).

> It had always been the purpose of God that man should live face to face with the divine perfection and reflect it in his own character; and the disastrous consequence of sin was that it removed man from the divine presence and so cut him off from the source of the glory he was designed to bear – 'all have sinned and fall short of the glory of God' (Rom. 3:23). This glory had been restored in Jesus, not only in the splendour of his risen power (2 Cor. 4:6), but also in the incognito of his earthly obedience (1 Cor. 2:8).

As the Epistle to the Hebrews insists, 'Son though he was, he learned obedience in the school of suffering, and, once perfected, became the source of eternal salvation for all who obey him' (Heb. 5:8f., NEB). His Sonship is mirrored in all the Gospels, not only in John; but perhaps the clearest picture of all 'is in the parable of the "Apprentice Son." A son can do nothing by himself; he does only what he sees

---

[6] Caird had previously emphasized the clear evidence for the fact that the resurrection, when it actually happened, took the disciples wholly by surprise.

his father doing: what the father does, the son does. For the father loves his son and shows him all that he is doing' (Jn. 5:19–20). And it is 'through the lens of this picture from daily life we are to see the relation between Jesus and God. So complete is the mutual understanding of this partnership that everything Jesus says or does is at the same time the word or deed of God' (p.14).

So much, in brief, for the historical evidence about the empty tomb, the resurrection appearances, and the experiential criteria which gave rise to the faith – and Christology – of the apostolic church. But at times it appears that some philosophers and theologians are more concerned with ideas than with data, and with their pet theories than with rational evidence.

Conclusion

In any case it was by the resurrection that Jesus was 'declared ['proclaimed', 'designated'] Son of God with power' (Rom. 1:4). This was basically by the act of God himself who – as the New Testament usually puts it – 'raised him from the dead'. No question of 'Adoptionism' arises – either at the resurrection, the baptism, or at any other time: the resurrection was an open manifestation of what Jesus had *always* been by nature. As Pannenberg puts it: 'If Jesus as a person is "the Son of God", as becomes clear retroactively from his resurrection, then he has always been the Son of God' (*Jesus: God and Man*, p.141). Still less was it the act of the early church, deifying their dead leader by 'changing the man Jesus into the god Christ'. It was precisely the opposite; for it was only because of what Jesus already was 'that the physical resurrection could take place, resurrection being the ultimate manifestation of his divinity and of the relationship of that divinity to humanity' (*cf.* Rachel Trickett, 'Imagination and Belief', p.3).

The fact that the New Testament usually states that it was God who 'raised Jesus' (or simply that Jesus 'was raised'), rather than that 'Jesus rose', might be thought to emphasize the power of God rather than the deity of the one he raised. After all, we believe that we ourselves will share in what Martha termed 'the resurrection at the last day' (Jn. 11:24).

But this is a very different matter from the unique resurrection of a particular person in the middle of history, which no Jew (in particular) would have ever envisaged. At the very least the fact that God acted in this way gives, as it were, the divine *imprimatur* to Jesus' deeds and words, and to the way in which he had often acted and spoken as only God himself could properly act or speak (*cf.* Pannenberg, p.67). Had he been anyone else, he would certainly (as his Jewish opponents believed and declared) have been a blasphemer; and would God have intervened in this unique way to vindicate a deliberate, or even a mistaken, blasphemer?

As for the church, C. F. D. Moule insists that, although the New Testament writers differ considerably among themselves in their conception of how, precisely, the exalted Christ was – and is – experienced by Christians, 'they all seem unanimously to reflect two convictions: first, that the Lord whom they revere and acclaim is continuous with the Jesus of Nazareth who had been crucified: none other than Jesus himself; and secondly, that he is transcendent and divine'. So he asks the pertinent question: 'If, subsequently to his death, he is conceived of as an eternally living being, personal but more than individual, one with God and the source of salvation, and if he is still firmly identified with Jesus of Nazareth, then what of his pre-existence? Can "eternal" personality existing after the incarnation be denied existence before it?'[7] More briefly, Pannenberg writes: 'Viewed from the confirmation of Jesus' claim by the resurrection, the inner logic of the matter dictates that Jesus was *always one with God,* not just after a certain date in his life' (*Jesus: God and Man,* p.153).

This somewhat lengthy – yet inevitably inadequate – discussion of the incarnation was occasioned by the fact that Hick himself recognizes that his 'Copernican revolution' in his theology of religion 'from a Christianity-centred or Jesus-centred to a God-centred model' necessarily involved 'a re-opening of the Christological question' (*cf.* pp.26, 28, above). This, as we have seen, is because he realizes that

if Jesus was literally God incarnate, the Second Person of the Holy Trinity living a human life, so that the Christian

[7] *Theologica Evangelica,* Vol. VIII, No. 3, Sept. 1975.

religion was founded by God-on-earth in person, it is then very hard to escape from the traditional view that all mankind must be converted to the Christian faith. However, the alternative possibility suggests itself that the idea of divine incarnation is to be understood metaphorically rather than literally.... As such, it should not be treated as a metaphysical truth from which we can draw further conclusions, such as that God's saving activity is confined to the single thread of human history documented in the Christian Bible (*God Has Many Names,* p.6).

Now there are several points here in which I should wish to express myself differently. To begin with, I should prefer the term 'God-in-manhood' to 'God-on-earth', in order to emphasize the essential difference between a Hindu *avatār* and a true incarnation (without any docetic implications). I should also wish to question what, precisely, Hick means when he asserts that 'all mankind must be converted to the Christian faith' or that 'God's saving activity' is as narrowly defined as his statement implies. I shall return to this subject in chapter 5. But with the nucleus of Hick's statement I whole-heartedly agree. If, as I believe, Jesus *was* God incarnate, and if what God himself did in Jesus at the cross of Calvary was to 'reconcile the world to himself', then Hick's concept of 'the great world religions as [merely] different human responses to the one divine Reality, embodying different perceptions which have been formed in different historical and cultural circumstances' is gravely inadequate. Like the religions themselves, it is a patchwork quilt of truth and error. Of course there are diversities of 'historical and cultural circumstances', in none of which God has 'left himself without witness'; and of course men and women have responded to this witness in a variety of different ways. But Jesus – with the salvation he came to announce, died to provide and lives to bring to final completion – stands on a pinnacle wholly by himself.[8]

The difference between this and the Theravāda form of Buddhism, for example, is brought out, H. D. Lewis insists, by the radically different attitudes taken by Jesus and the

[8] For further comments on Hick's views, see my *Mystery of the Incarnation,* ch. 3.

Buddha to the significance of their persons and what they came to do.

> When Buddha, at the time of his death, was asked how it would be best to remember him he simply urged his followers not to trouble themselves about such a question. It did not matter much whether they remembered him or not, the essential thing was the teaching – and what mattered about the teaching was the *Way*, to live so that at last, in this life or later, illumination and release would be ours too. It is almost, in this regard, like a scientific doctrine; it does not matter all that who propounded it provided we can understand it and use it now. Its importance is in no way bound up with the way it was discovered. We can understand it without knowing anything of its inventor. But this is not the way of Christian truth (*World Religions*, p.174).

This, on the contrary, is focused in the person of Jesus and in the historical fact of his death and resurrection; so we 'find that Jesus, the embodiment of self-denial and humility, also puts Himself at the centre of redeeming activity. He is Himself the way, the truth and the life, and His disciples, far from forgetting who He was or what He did Himself, are to come to Him, to be drawn to Him, and in sacramental worship to "Do this in remembrance of Me"' (*World Religions*, p.174). It is deeply significant, moreover, that this remembrance was to be specifically in terms of his atoning death.

Other religions may, indeed, include the belief that God, or one of the gods, manifested himself once, or many times, in human form, or that some 'divine light-substance' has passed from one individual to a succession of others. But Christianity alone has dared to claim that 'the one, omnipotent, omniscient Ground of all existence' has uniquely intervened in his creation, not by assuming the mere form or appearance of a man, but by actually becoming incarnate; not by living and teaching alone, but by actually dying a felon's death 'for us men and for our salvation'; and by putting his seal on the fact and efficacy of this intervention by rising again from the dead. This, in the apostolic proclamation, constituted the unique event which was the culmination of all that had gone before and the beginning of a new age. The kingdom had come with power (*cf.* E. O. James, *Christianity and Other Religions*, pp.66, 166).

3

A unique salvation?

Introduction

My last chapter was concerned with the *kerygma* with which the apostolic church burst upon the world, with its triumphant – and, indeed, irrepressible – proclamation that Jesus of Nazareth was not only the Jewish Messiah but a divine Saviour. We saw that the very foundation and substance of this proclamation was a unique event – the life, death and resurrection of a historical person; and that this was recorded at a time when a large number of those who had actually known him were still alive, many of whom could testify to a personal experience of having met the risen Christ.

It must now be our task to examine in rather more detail the significance of this unique historical event as expounded by the apostolic church, first from the point of view of the new quality of life which characterized those who received the proclamation, and then from that of the new insight into the nature and character of God which it opened up. In the first of these studies we shall be concerned with the Christian understanding of the purpose and goal of human existence, as compared with that of other religions and ideologies; and in the second we shall turn to the basic beliefs which lie behind all religions and ideologies regarding the reality, and nature, of the transcendent.

For my present subject I have chosen, after considerable

hesitation, the title 'A unique salvation?'. I am aware, of course, that the word 'salvation' may seem somewhat traditional or even hackneyed; but I have chosen it because it seems to me more comprehensive than any of the other terms which might be used instead. It includes, according to the *Oxford English Dictionary*, both the 'state or fact of being saved', and the 'action of saving or delivering', so it will comprehend in its scope both what 'salvation' signifies in different religions and ideologies and also the means by which this salvation is achieved or received. It also properly covers both man's life here on earth and what may await him after life in this world, as we know it, has come to an end.

The basic meaning of the term, as I understand it, is that of deliverance or release. In terms of this life this means to be saved or delivered from sickness, calamity, injustice, oppression, false attitudes, ignorance or sin; and in terms of the hereafter to deliverance from judgment, loss, separation from God or an endless cycle of re-incarnations. In essence, therefore, the word salvation means that a man is 'saved' or kept *from* something; but this necessarily leads, by implication at least, to the more positive concept that one delivered or preserved from sickness of body or soul is thereby made, or kept, healthy and 'whole', and that one saved from judgment after death, or set free from re-incarnation, is thereby admitted to future bliss – whether this is conceived in terms of 'heaven' or of release from individuality and the cessation of desire.

The first and most obvious distinction, then, is between those religions or ideologies which concentrate exclusively on this life; those which are concerned predominantly with the eternal world as they conceive this to be; and those which put a real – if not necessarily equal – emphasis on both. Another basic division is between those religions which teach that salvation must be achieved or earned and those which emphasize that it can never be won but only received – together, of course, with how it is to be achieved or received, as the case may be. Another way of putting a similar, but by no means identical, distinction would be to divide religions into those characterized by law and those characterized by redemption. And whichever classification is used, this must necessarily involve a discussion of the widespread, but equally varied and even contradictory, concept of sacrifice or expiation found in so many different religions.

Salvation in terms of this world

Political religions

First, then, those religions and ideologies which postulate man's salvation – whether or not they would ever use that word – primarily or exclusively in terms of this world. Here we think, first, of the great ideologies which are embraced and followed today with quasi-religious devotion, and can almost be termed 'political religions'. There can be little doubt that some of the most dynamic forces in contemporary society are to be found in movements which are primarily political rather than religious, for Communism, Fascism and various forms of Nationalism have shown themselves able to move men's hearts, minds and wills on a scale that few purely religious movements have done in recent years (*cf.* Dewick, p.5). This is not to suggest that these movements have influenced individuals more profoundly or effectively than has religious conviction, but rather that their power to evoke self-sacrifice and passionate devotion has been more widespread. Indeed, these movements possess, in Hendrick Kraemer's phrase, 'all the paraphernalia of religion'.

Thus Harold Laski described Stalin and his associates as 'men who have a conviction that is religious in its profundity. They have a "vision" of its character. They are convinced that it is infinitely precious. They believe that no sacrifices are too great for its attainment. . . . They believe that the only sin is weakness, that error is as profound a threat to victory as was heresy to the Christian of an earlier age. Their effort has for them all the elements of a crusade. . . . The Bolshevik, not less than the Puritan, is guided by his Inner Light. . . . The Bolshevik reliance upon their texts from Marx and Lenin and Stalin is identical with the Puritan dependence upon citations from the Scriptures' (Laski, pp.71ff.).

The same writer described the devotion of the German

people to their Führer in these terms: 'Worship of the Leader is made into a cult. Hitler is the Chosen of God, omniscient, infallible, the Father of his people, half ruler, half priest. . . . His officials express themselves as missionaries of a faith, the power of which is beyond human ken. Its origin is wrapped in mystery, it is not subject to the scrutiny of ordinary rational processes' (Laski, p.119).

Similarly, in Nkrumah's Ghana, his title of 'Osagyefo' could be (and no doubt was) interpreted as 'National Deliverer' by the more sophisticated, but was understood simply as 'Redeemer' by others; and I myself once heard choruses, which I had learnt as a boy to sing in praise of Christ, being chanted by Nkrumah's followers in his honour, with the minimum of verbal change.

In the case of Communism, this vision for which men are prepared to sacrifice everything is (with few exceptions) defined exclusively in terms of this life – to bring men, that is, deliverance from exploitation, poverty and social injustice and to substitute a new structure and ethos of society in which all men make their contribution to the common good without fear of want or the incentive of personal gain. It has almost always been coupled with an explicit atheism and a forthright denunciation of religion as the 'opiate of the people' which is exploited by the 'Establishment' to make the working classes content with miserable conditions here on earth in the hope of 'pie in the sky when they die'. And while it is true that both Mussolini and Hitler were not averse to invoking the name of God on occasion, as a hypocritical pandering to political convenience, it is clear that Fascism does not differ fundamentally from Communism in this regard.

Stephen Neill has pointed out that while Marx seems to have accepted the thesis of D. F. Strauss, that Christianity rested on a myth created by the suppressed Christian community of the decaying Roman Empire around the supposedly historical figure of Jesus of Nazareth, yet he was 'never able to escape from the world of the Bible. His own thought seems all the time to move in the same realms as the hopes of the prophets of the Old Testament and the eschatological expectations of the writers of the New. There is a biblical drama in which God is the chief actor. The

Marxist picture seems to be a secularized version of the same drama with the principal actor left out.' So in place of the Kingdom of God there is to be 'a kingdom of man, in which oppression will wither away and man, delivered from his alienation against himself, will live in peace with himself and his brother'. Nor will this kingdom ever be established by the gradual victory of justice over injustice, but only by the violent revolution of man – rather than the decisive intervention of God. There is even 'a sinless victim, the proletariat, through whose sufferings the exploiters of the past have made themselves rich', but whose agony is to end in triumph – to take the place of the Jesus on whom the sins of others were laid but whose sufferings will usher in a new world in which he will be exalted (Neill, pp.154f.). And Leslie Lyall has shown how the parallels to biblical concepts have not ended with Marx himself, for in China the Communist emphasis on confession of errors, followed by brainwashing, simulate Christian repentance and conversion (Lyall, pp.69f.).

The basic fallacy in this is not the emphasis on the exploitation of the proletariat in the past – and still, in part, today. This is sad and sober fact; and Marx was right to insist that this must not only be recognized, but changed. The fallacy lies, rather, partly in the myth of the 'sinlessness' of the proletariat, and the illusion that, were exploitation by the upper classes brought to an end, then discord, crime and sin would disappear and the golden age would dawn; and partly in the materialistic philosophy which thinks that every problem has an economic solution. Man, the Christian insists, was made in the 'image and likeness' of God, so the essential value of the individual must never be debased to the position of a cog in a state machine. But man is now a fallen creature, in whom the image and likeness of God, while still present, has been grievously marred and distorted; so it is not only society which needs a change in its economic structure, but the individual who needs a radical spiritual transformation. This is something the gospel of Marx cannot effect. And, without this transformation, a revolution against one unjust regime is as likely to establish another equally tyrannical form of government in its place as it is to effect any lasting reform.

The Sadducees and some Buddhist groups

But an exclusive emphasis on this life is not confined to the
'political religions'. It was also largely characteristic of the
Sadducees. Whether they were mainly a political or a religious party, a rural aristocracy or state officials, they did
not believe in angels, demons or the resurrection. Instead,
they put all their emphasis on the Pentateuch; and they
taught that obedience to the Law led to prosperity and
blessing, and disobedience led to adversity and loss, here
on earth. And although the Pharisees took a very different
attitude to the immortality of the soul, it is clear that the
primary emphasis in the Old Testament itself is on this life
rather than the hereafter (*cf.* Gelson, p.1368; Ellison, p.120).

Theravāda and Zen Buddhism

What may, perhaps, appear to be a primary concern with
this present life may also be found in Theravāda Buddhism.
It was the misery and mystery of suffering that prompted
Gautama to abandon a life of ease and family happiness,
first for that of the contemporary discipline of the ascetic
path, and then for that of solitary contemplation; and it was
his perception of the solution to the problem of suffering
that represented the core of his 'Enlightenment'. What he
perceived can best be expressed in terms of the 'Four Aryan
Truths'. The first is the Truth of Anguish – that suffering is
intrinsic to all human experience. The second is the Truth
of the Arising of Anguish – that it comes from a desire to
possess, to be and to become that amounts to a positive
craving (*tanhā*). The third is the Truth of the Stopping of
Anguish – that the only way of escape is by a firm resolve to
have done with all attachment to, and craving for, the
transient, and to embrace in their place the fourth Aryan
Truth, which consists in the discipline of the Aryan Eightfold Path. This alone can lead man to *Nirvāna,* a state of
passionless peace, which is the ultimate goal of all Buddhist
teaching. With its realization Gautama became the Buddha;
and at this point he could have ended his earthly pilgrimage.
But instead he made the noble choice, out of compassion
for suffering humanity, to set out on a wandering ministry

of instruction and to found a monastic Order (Samgha) to perpetuate his teaching.

But Theravāda Buddhists in practice believe that the goal of *Nirvāna*, which represents their concept of 'Salvation', is seldom, if ever, reached until after an indefinite number of re-births (past or future) – although the Buddhist teaching about rebirth is far more complex and difficult to comprehend than the Hindu doctrine on this subject, since Buddhists (unlike Hindus) deny that there is any eternal 'soul' or 'self' to be re-incarnated. What they believe is that desire, if not eliminated, always generates another being which inherits the *karma*, or accumulation of merit and demerit, of the person (or even some other person) who has died – and that it is possible for this being, in certain states of mind, to remember, in part, the former existence from which this *karma* was inherited (*cf.* Eliot, Vol. I, pp. 191–198).

In practice, therefore, it is chiefly in Zen Buddhism – which originally sprang from the Mahāyāna rather than the Theravāda branch of Buddhism – that the door is held wide open to the attainment of this enlightenment in this present life. In regard to the *means* to that end, Zen Buddhists stand firmly with Theravādins in insisting that man must 'work out his own salvation' by his own efforts rather than rely on any such outside aid as that to which the various sects of Mahāyāna Buddhism commonly turn. Where Zen Buddhists differ from the Theravādins, even in this respect, is in positing 'an enlightenment or intuitive grasp of the truth not only at the end of the Path, but here and now, as they persevere on the Path itself' (Lewis and Slater, p. 76). Zen is the Japanese form of the Chinese Ch'an, which itself is a translation of the Sanscrit *dhyāna*, or meditation; and Zen Buddhists believe that by rigorous self-discipline and a strictly prescribed method of meditation they may attain *satori*, the Japanese term for 'enlightenment' – whether suddenly, as some teach, or gradually, as others hold – by means of a perception which is empirical rather than intellectual. In some respects, then, they have a considerable affinity with contemporary existentialists. Naturally enough (seeing that Buddhism emerged from the bosom of Hinduism) there are also close parallels with *yoga* techniques and teaching – except for the pervasive Hindu emphasis on re-incarnation.

Salvation primarily in terms of eternity

Hinduism

So we turn next to those religions which put a predominant emphasis not on this life, with its suffering, injustice and evil, but on what lies beyond the grave. And here we must give pride of place to Hinduism. To the Advaita Vedānta school of Hindu philosophy, for example, there is only one Absolute Reality, and all else – this phenomenal universe, and all that goes with it – is, in the ultimate sense, only *māyā*, 'illusion' or 'appearance'. It may indeed be said that the great theme of nearly all schools of Hindu thought is: 'Turn where we will, nothing in present existence is permanent. The Wheel of Life revolves, with sentient beings passing from one existence to another, be it as men or as gods or animals, be it on this earth or elsewhere, in the migratory *samsāra* process. Nor is this by chance. What is reaped is what has been sown. What has been enacted in some distant past affects what is possible in the present, according to the law of *karma*' (Lewis and Slater, p.61). (This may, in part, explain a certain lack of compassion in Hinduism, since misery and destitution – to say nothing of caste – may be ascribed to the inevitable outworking of *karma*.) The all-important goal is a changeless condition of 'peace and rest', for to the Hindu 'salvation' means *moksha*, and '*moksha*, as usually understood, means salvation or liberation not from moral guilt but from the human condition as such – it is liberation from space and time, and the felt experience of immortality' (Zaehner, *Hinduism*, p.138).

In essence, as Zaehner puts it, the Upanishads teach 'that the human soul in its deepest essence is in some sense identical with Brahman, the unchanging something that is yet the source of all change. This soul, then, must be distinct from the ordinary empirical self which transmigrates from body to body carrying its load of *karma* with it. How to realise this eternal soul and how to disengage it from its real or imaginary connection with the psychosomatic complex that thinks, wills and acts, is from the time of the Upanishads onwards the crucial problem facing the Hindu religious consciousness' (*Hinduism*, p.60). But there were six different schools of thought. To Sankara and his Advaita Vedānta school *moksha* 'does not mean that the soul merges into Brahman as a river merges into the sea, but that it realises itself as it eternally is, that is, as the One Brahman–Ātman, which is Absolute Being, Consciousness and Bliss. With the realisation of this, *māyā* disappears. . . . Real and verifiable from the point of view of the soul still in bondage to matter, it is unreal to the soul which has realised the true oneness of itself.' Sankara 'does not deny the existence of the Creator God on the empirical level nor does he identify the soul with this God on any level. . . . But from the absolute point of view *māyā* does not exist; so man and God must be identically Brahman'. This state, he asserts, is 'unthinkable' and 'cannot be designated. Its essence is the firm conviction of the oneness of itself; *it causes the phenomenal world to cease*; it is tranquil and mild, devoid of duality' (Zaehner, *Hinduism*, pp.75ff. His italics).

By contrast, the Sāmkhya and Yoga schools, which are often coupled together, are frankly dualist. To them *moksha* 'does *not* mean to see all things in the self and the self in all things; it means rather to *isolate* the self or soul – and the self is not a universal, all-pervading Self or World-Soul, but one self among countless others – from all other things, both the whole samsāric world and all other "selves" which, like itself, are self-subsisting and autarchic monads'. The Sāmkhya system proper 'admits of no God'. But another way of putting this is to say that God 'is no different from other souls in that he is eternal and unlimited by time, since that is the natural condition of all souls, but he *is* different from them in that he is never affected by matter or Nature . . . *Moksha*, then, for the Sāmkhya-Yogin, means to become *like* God in his timeless unity, it does not mean to participate in him in any way. The goal is isolation, not union or fusion as in the Upanishadic concept of merging into Brahman' (Zaehner, *Hinduism*, pp.69ff.).

These Hindu schools of philosophy, then, are all virtually atheistic in essence – as are also Theravāda Buddhism and Jainism. To the Jain 'salvation is to be found by freeing the soul from matter, so that the former may enjoy omniscient self-sufficient bliss for all eternity'. To attain salvation, therefore, a man must 'subject himself to rigorous hardship and pain to get rid of *karma* already acquired, and act with the utmost circumspection lest he acquire new *karma* in serious quantities' – for in Jainism *karma* is 'conceived on the analogy of a material substance' (Basham, 'Jainism', pp.256f.).

In Theravāda Buddhism, on the other hand, people go to monks and monasteries to be instructed in the *dharma*[1] or teaching of the Buddha; and 'while they do not, or should not, pray to the Buddha they may very well love to have before them the representation of some image of their Master which enables them to think of his virtues, his love and his compassion'. As a Burmese scholar put it: 'The words they recite are meditations and not prayers. They recite to themselves the virtues of the Buddha, his Dhamma [Pali for the Sanscrit *dharma*] and his Holy Order (*Samgha*)', which here 'stands, ideally, only for . . . those wearers of the yellow robe who have complete mastery in moral behaviour, concentration, wisdom, freedom and the knowledge of and insight into freedom' – that is, the more advanced 'Arhants' (*cf.* Horner, p.290).

In the West, the Buddhist *Nirvāna* – at least when conceived in terms of Theravāda teaching – has often been equated with annihilation; but this has been challenged by Buddhists. Literally the term simply means 'nakedness' or 'emptiness'; and Buddhists are wont to insist that 'what is extinguished is not life itself but the craving and vain attachments which must indeed be destroyed if nirvana . . . is to be attained'. Again, *Nirvāna*, although usually described in negative terms, is sometimes depicted by Mahāyāna Buddhists as 'the further shore, the harbour of refuge, the cool cave, the matchless island, the holy city. It is sheer bliss.' This raises a number of problems to the student of Buddhism. It has been said, for instance, that 'What we apprehend as human existence belongs to the realm of *anicca*, the impermanent and perpetually changing, in which there is no abiding reality. Such a realm is neces-

---

[1] This term essentially means the 'law' or standard of conduct to which a man has a duty to conform.

sarily *anatta*, 'without soul' [or 'self']; there can be no place in it for a permanent centre of human consciousness. Man is not a unity; he is simply the coalescence of five *khandās*[2] which happen to come together' (Neill, pp.107ff.). When they coalesce they produce the illusion of an existing self; but this temporary coalescence ends at death. So what then?

This is why people often ask: 'Who is it that enjoys *Nirvāna* if there is not much left of the man so-and-so after he has died?' To this I. B. Horner replies: 'The question framed thus is inept and does not fit. Rather should it be asked: Who enjoys *Nirvāna* here and now? The answer is the adept in meditation. For *Nirvāna* may be seen in this very life.' There are, he says, four stages on the way to Arhantship or *Nirvāna*. In the first stage the aspirant becomes certain of ultimately attaining enlightenment. He will never be reborn as other than a human being – and, even so, seven times at most. In the second stage he has advanced so far that he will return only once more to birth as a human being, and will then make an end of anguish. At the third stage he will never be reborn on earth, but 'after his death here will become a denizen of one of the highest *deva*[3]-worlds and attain *Nirvāna* there when the residual *karma* that led to this *deva*-birth has expended itself'. So the fourth stage is that of Arhantship itself, in which he has reached final liberation here and attains *parinirvāna*, in which state he will subsist until his body dies (*cf.* Horner, pp.290ff.). But at this point we must, I think, leave this subject for the present, and turn to the more theistic forms of Hinduism and Buddhism – except to observe that I believe Zaehner is right in classifying the knowledge or enlightenment claimed by Advaita Vedānta Hindus and Theravāda Buddhists as falling within the category of 'nature' or 'monistic', rather than theistic, mysticism.[4]

---

[2] These five are made up of the physical body, together with feeling, perception, volitional activities (or habitual tendencies) and consciousness (Horner, p.280).

[3] The root meaning of the word is to shine; and a *deva* is neither an animal nor a man, but a being regarded as in some ways above the human level – yet *not*, properly, as any sort of God.

[4] But *cf.* Davis, pp.93–97; Lewis and Slater, pp.166–169.

Hindus of the bhakti *persuasion*

But whatever view may be taken by the schools of Hindu philosophy, there can be little doubt that the average Indian today has a far more theistic approach to religion. The ordinary villager probably envisages a number of different gods, one of whom he regards as the special deity of his clan or locality, while more sophisticated persons tend to think in terms of one supreme God who can be worshipped under a number of different names or forms, and has revealed himself in a variety of *avatārs*, or theophanies. There have also been several *bhakti* movements characterized by personal devotion to some deity. This feature of Hinduism can be traced back at least to the Tamil-speaking Ālgārs of the seventh century AD who were devotees of Vishnu; but the *bhakti* movement, which spread in various forms all over India, probably reached its zenith in Rāmānuja, a Tamil Brāhman of the eleventh century. He claimed to be a Vedāntin, but declared 'that Śankara's teaching leads to a state of bliss below the highest, which is only gained by intense devotion to God', and that salvation is 'gained by completely abandoning oneself into the hands of God and humbly waiting for his grace, which will never be refused' (Basham, 'Hinduism', p.234). Whereas to Śankara *bhakti* is a very inferior substitute, or preliminary stage, on the way to knowledge (*jñāna*), or the realization of absolute unity, to Rāmānuja liberation is no more than the transcendence of time and space, which is the birthright of every human soul. The love of God, he taught, 'is a different and entirely new experience, and it takes place in eternity not in time. Liberation may be an excellent thing, but compared to the love of God it is as a mustard seed beside Mount Meru, and the selfish cultivation of one's own immortal soul is contemptuously dismissed as fit only for those who do not know how to love' (Zaehner, *Hinduism*, p.100). Among the greatest of his successors was Rāmānanda, and among the latter's followers was Kabīr, one of the world's greatest religious poets (Zaehner, pp.139f.)

But it is only in the hymns of the Tamil-speaking devotees

of Śiva,[5] as distinct from their Vaishnavite counterparts, that we find 'the extreme sense of unworthiness that the devotee feels in the face of the all-holiness of God'. It was the influence of these Tamil saints that 'made the writers of the *Śaiva-Siddhānta* attach such enormous importance to the doctrine of grace freely given and the impossibility of spiritual progress without love. The whole movement is an impassioned cry against the ossified ceremonial religion of the Brāhmans and the ideal of passionlessness that they shared with the Buddhists and the Jains' (Zaehner, pp.130f.). Yet the picture of Śiva we get in Klaus Klostermaier's *Hindu and Christian in Vrindaban* is very different (*cf.* my *God's Law and God's Love*, pp.20f.): 'When misfortune goes on increasing, when catastrophe breaks all bounds, it is imperative to sacrifice to the goddess; her long tongue hangs bloodthirstily from her mouth, she holds a bloodstained sword, cut-off heads and arms are hanging decoratively over her naked breasts. Life issues from God's countenance, death from his back.' One could hardly find a more vivid picture of the varieties of beliefs and practices which come under the exceedingly wide umbrella of Hinduism.

Mahāyāna Buddhism

Much the same applies to Buddhism. We have already discussed some of the tenets of its original, Theravādic form. But in the lands of south-east Asia and the Far East it was the teaching of the Mahāyāna (the 'Great Vehicle', as distinct from the Hīnayāna, or the 'Small Vehicle' – as they call the Theravāda, or 'doctrine of the elders') which spread most widely. The Four Aryan Truths, the Eightfold Aryan Path and a belief in *Nirvāna* as the goal are common to both branches of Buddhism; but the Mahāyāna, in its various sects, is chiefly distinguished by its emphasis on compassion, on its promise of outside aid in the form of Bodhisattvas (and Buddhas) to help man on his way, and on its elaboration of the meaning of *Nirvāna*. In point of time the rise of the Mahāyāna coincides with the beginning of the

[5] Ultimately, sophisticated Hindus regard Vishnu, Śiva *et al.* as different aspects of one God.

Christian era and certain contacts between Greece and India — a fact that may have considerable significance. It was probably to the creation of the Bodhisattva ideal that the Mahāyāna owed most of its success; for a Bodhisattva is a being who is depicted as motivated by two ideals: on the one hand to win full enlightenment and become a Buddha, and on the other to help suffering humanity, for which he is prepared selflessly to postpone his own entrance into *Nirvāna* (Conze, pp.293, 297ff.).

This is not the place to attempt to describe all the sects and ramifications of Mahāyāna Buddhism, and I must confine myself to a few distinctly extreme examples. We have already seen something of Zen Buddhism, so we must now consider Pure Land Buddhism, in which the view of 'enlightenment' and of the means of attaining it are both about as far removed from those of the Zen sect — or, indeed, the Theravāda branch of Buddhism — as they could possibly be. In place of 'sweltering at the task' of self-effort, Pure Land Buddhists are taught to put their faith unreservedly in a Bodhisattva (long since become a Buddha) named Amitābha (or Amida), who fills the role of a virtually divine Saviour to his followers. He presides over a Pure (or Buddha) Land named Sukhāvatī, situated far away in the Western quarter of the universe; and, because of his great vows, infinite merit and unlimited power to save, those who rely on his grace attain at once a measure of enlightenment and are certain to be re-born in Sukhāvatī.

They could never, in these degenerate days of the 'Counterfeit Law', have achieved this through their own efforts — as may have been possible for people who took the Saintly Road in the period of the True Law. Instead, taking the 'Easy Road', they must invoke the help of Amitābha which will ensure their entrance into this Pure Land where there are 'trees of gold, silver, lapis lazuli, crystal and coral'. But this is not a picture of sensual delights, for 'while rich banquets may be spread, none partake of them'. That Buddha country is 'pure and peaceful.... It is like the Uncreate and is like *Nirvāna* itself' (Lewis and Slater, p.80). In a very early text it is regarded as a paradise whose inhabitants live in unbroken happiness until they obtain *Nirvāna*; but in popular esteem, Eliot writes, 'it is virtually equivalent to heaven' (Eliot, Vol. II, pp.29ff.). As Charles Davis puts it, conditions there 'were more favourable for the attainment of *Nirvāna*', and hope of reception into it 'took the place for some of *Nirvāna* as a goal' (p.106). Was it, then, regarded primarily as a launching-pad, or as a substitute, for *Nirvāna*?

The next Mahāyāna sect to which I must devote a few lines is that of Lamaism, as this developed in Tibet. This is of particular interest in this context for two reasons. First, because it emerged after a long struggle with the indigenous Bon religion – and so provides an example of the way Mahāyāna Buddhism has often absorbed or become amalgamated with other beliefs and practices (Confucianism, Taoism, Tantrism, Shintō, *etc.*). Secondly, because it demonstrates in practice the belief that developed in Living Buddhas who could assume, at their will, a 'phantom body'. This illustrates the philosophical synthesis between the divergent forms of Buddhism which the Samgha evolved in the 'Three-Body' doctrine, in which a Buddha exists on three different levels. On the human level he has a 'transformation-body' which is fictitious or 'conjured up'. On the 'heavenly' level he has an 'enjoyment-body', or body of spiritual bliss. And at the deepest level he has a 'Dharma-body', a body of 'truth, essence, being'. At that level Buddha means the 'impersonal, undifferentiated Absolute or Ultimate' – a form in which Mahāyāna Buddhism 'is similar in structure to Advaita Vedānta' (*cf.* Davis, pp.106f.).

Finally, we must return to the concept of *Nirvāna*. It is in this context that Conze writes about 'the phantasmagoria' of the Mahāyāna 'world of illusion'. For in reality, he says,

there are no Buddhas, no Bodhisattvas, no perfections, no stages, and no paradises – none of all this. All these conceptions have no reference to anything that is actually there, and concern a world of mere phantasy. They are just expedients, concessions to the multitude of the ignorant, provisional constructions of thought, which become superfluous after having served their purpose. For the Mahāyāna is a 'vehicle', designed to ferry people across to salvation. When the goal of the Beyond has been reached, it can safely be discarded (Conze, p.309).

As for the Beyond itself, this has been described as 'Emptiness,' 'Suchness', and the 'One'. 'Emptiness', we are told, 'means an absolute transcendental reality beyond the grasp of intellectual comprehension and verbal expression.... The attitude of the perfected sage is one of non-assertion.' It is called 'Suchness', again, 'if and when we take it "such as it is", without adding anything to it or subtracting anything from it'; and it is the 'One' because 'it alone is real'.

The attempt to define this ultimate reality led to two schools of thought. One school held that 'no positive statement whatsoever can be made about the Absolute' and that 'the Buddha's "roaring silence" is the only medium by which it can be communicated', while the other believed that it could be described as 'Mind', 'Thought' or 'Consciousness'. The first view, Conze remarks, is 'primarily a logical doctrine, which by the successive self-annihilation of all propositions arrives at an all-embracing scepticism' (of which he regards Kant as the nearest European exponent); the second, he says, is a 'philosophy of metaphysical idealism, which teaches that consciousness can exist by itself without an object, and that it creates its objects out of its own inner potentialities' (of which he considers the thought of Berkeley to be 'the nearest European equivalent'). In other words, the first school believes that 'salvation is attained when everything has been dropped, and absolute Emptiness alone remains', while to the other 'salvation means to have "an act of cognition which no longer apprehends an object", an act of thought which is "Thought-only"' (Conze, pp.312f.).

The description of the 'Pure Land' quoted above is reminiscent, in part, of the word-pictures of Paradise given in the Qur'ān and even of the Heavenly City in the book of Revelation. There have, moreover, been both Muslims and Christians who have regarded life here on earth as of very little importance, and the attainment of Paradise or heaven as the only matter of any real significance. Such were those Muslims who positively welcomed death in the Holy War, and those Christians who actively sought martyrdom. But the central strand of Christian and Muslim – as also of Zoroastrian – teaching is much more balanced, and regards both life on earth and life beyond the grave as of real, if not equal, importance. So it is to this view of 'salvation' that we must now turn.

'Salvation' in terms both of this life and eternity

Zoroastrianism puts a major emphasis on the importance of both ceremonial and moral purity in this world in the light of the judgment of the world to come, with its punishment for the wicked and reward for the righteous. Immortality is a constant theme in the Zoroastrian scriptures, together with the narrow Chinvat bridge which separates the good from the evil; and heaven is the reward for righteousness, while hell is described as an 'age-long and lonely misery of punishment for liars'. In Islam, too, a primary place is always given to the sacred law, the Sharī'a, which prescribes in the utmost detail those divine commands and prohibitions which constitute the authoritative blue-print for the life of the individual Muslim – and, indeed, the Islamic State – here on earth; but this is invariably given in the context of the Day of Judgment, which will bring the ultimate sanction for every transgression and omission. And much the same is true of Judaism.[6]

This dual emphasis on this world and the next is also, of course, characteristic of New Testament Christianity. Christian doctrine can never be exclusively concerned with the transcendent world in view of the fact that when the eternal Word 'was made flesh' God himself became 'very man'. Jesus taught, moreover, that men and women can be 'born again', or 'born from above', here in this world; so eternal life for the Christian begins here and now – although it will certainly become fuller and richer in the world to come. Christianity too, like Islam, believes in the 'resurrection of the body'; but whereas the Qur'ān usually seems to depict this in frankly physical terms, the New Testament teaches that the dead will rise again not as mere disembodied spirits, on the one hand, nor with physical bodies,

---

[6] For a more adequate treatment, *cf.* my *God's Law and God's Love* (chs. 2 and 3).

on the other, but with new 'spiritual bodies' (1 Cor. 15:35–50). And while this life lasts the Christian is required to act as the salt and the light of the community in which he lives, to fulfil all a citizen's duties, to love his neighbour as himself, and yet to remember that his true citizenship is in heaven, where his 'treasure' should always be (for there he will 'see the King in his beauty', be conformed to the likeness of Christ, and 'be for ever with the Lord'). So Christianity, as Michael Ramsey has put it, is intensely other-worldly and at the same time thoroughly down to earth, requiring a dual allegiance to the sacred and the secular (*Sacred and Secular*, pp.6ff.).

The Christian concept of salvation, moreover, is not restricted to what happens to the individual soul after death. The New Testament picture of the meaning of salvation includes what Lesslie Newbigin calls

> the great corporate and cosmic completion of God's work in Christ, whereby all things will be restored to the unity for which they were created in Christ, and God will be all in all. In that final consummation the whole history of the world, as well as the history of each human soul, will find its true end. To be saved is to participate – in fore-taste now and in fulness at the end – in this final victory of Christ. According to the New Testament, the coming of Christ, his dying and rising and ascension, is the decisive moment in God's plan of salvation, presenting to every man who hears of it the opportunity and the necessity for faith, repentance, conversion and commitment to participation in the work of God in this present age.

To refuse this opportunity, and thereby to forgo the possibility of salvation, is to be 'lost' (*The Finality of Christ*, pp.60f.).

How then can 'salvation' be attained?

In distinguishing the various sects and schools of thought which jostle each other under the broad umbrellas of Hinduism and Buddhism, for example, I have almost inevitably anticipated this vital point. But we must now try to draw together the heterogeneous answers without too much repetition. Clearly enough, in some religions or schools of thought 'salvation' must be achieved, won or attained by the one who is 'saved' – by the moral quality of his life, the degree of illumination he achieves, the merit of the sacrifices he offers, or the depth of his religious commitment. In others 'salvation' can never be earned by man, but can come only from some divine 'Saviour'.

Primal religions

In primal religions there is always, I think, a recognition of a High or Creator God, as we shall see in our next chapter; but man is much more intimately concerned with a multitude of far more immanent spirits – good and bad, beneficent and malignant. These may, or may not, be identified with the souls of the dead. In primitive tribes there is little apprehension of 'good' and evil' as abstract ethical standards, but there is a vivid sense of the individual's participation in the life of his tribe or family – including, as we have already noted, both the dead and the yet unborn. A man's primary duty is to preserve and strengthen the 'vital force' of his tribe, for on this its happiness and prosperity depend, and to take all necessary steps to ward off the loss or diminution of vital force which would result from any infringement of the rules and taboos by which tribal life is hedged about. If he fails to take such steps the retribution will be terrible. As a result, primal religions are, above all, characterized by fear. Rituals must be performed to ward off the evil influence of those souls of the dead and other spirits which are regarded as dangerous, and to conserve the vital force of those ancestors whose influence is benign. And the dependence of the living on the dead is matched by that of the dead on the living (Neill, pp.133ff.). So the gifts, sacrifices and libations so characteristic of primal religions – including, in some cases, even human sacrifice – are regarded as absolutely necessary to ward off evil and calamity and to preserve the life-force of both the living and the dead; and in this preservation lies their conception of 'salvation'.

Hinduism

When we turn to Hinduism we find a much higher and more sophisticated realm of ideas. Starting with the comparatively simple doctrine of the Veda, *yajña* (sacrifice) and *karma* (religious rites, or action in general terms) are regarded as the means by which 'salvation' is attained (*cf.* Eliot, Vol. I, p.68). This becomes, in the understanding of a recent Hindu writer, the concept that 'life is a continual transaction between the gods and men in which man offers ceremonial gifts to the gods from the gifts they have bestowed on him and in return is enriched, protected, fostered.... Even salvation, even the highest good is to be gained by ceremonial sacrifice' (Aurobindo, pp.104f.).

But in the much more complex doctrine of the Upanishads and the Gītā release from space, time and the ever-repeated re-incarnations which the *karma,* or actions (whether good or bad), of the past and present inevitably entail, can be achieved only in one of several different ways: by fulfilling not only the temporal *dharma,* or duty, of one's caste but the eternal *dharma* which is still more fundamental[7]; by practising the rigorous discipline of the Yoga technique and teaching; by coming to realize that individuality and all 'duality' is an illusion, and that there is in fact only One without any second, the 'One Brahman-Ātman which is Absolute Being, Consciousness and Bliss'; or by attaining, after liberation, to a state of unification – but *not* identification – with a personal God (*cf.* Zaehner, *Hinduism,* pp.96, 124, 70ff., 75ff. and 78f.). So salvation, to the Hindu, is attained – though very rarely, it would seem – by way of righteousness (or the eternal *dharma*); much more frequently by means of asceticism *(tapas)* and Yoga disciplines; by knowledge *(jñāna)* attained through the practice of virtue, piety and meditation; or by devotion *(bhakti)* to some god or gods. Any of these are means by which union with Brahman, however this term may be defined, may ultimately be achieved. Innumerable examples could be given of the earnestness with which many Hindus seek this

---

[7] Particularly in the eyes of Hindu reformers such as Gandhi. *Cf.* J. N. D. Anderson, 'Reflections on Law: Natural, Divine and Positive', pp.17ff. (and *passim*) and Inaugural Lecture, pp.19f. (and *passim*).

salvation (for themselves or even for others) in a variety of different ways (*cf.* Klostermaier, pp.20f.).

Yet in Hinduism we also get glimpses of the intervention of a saviour-god. This is particularly true of the picture of Krishna in the Gītā (which has come largely to dominate popular Hinduism), as may be illustrated by the story of how he several times saved cowherds from a forest fire which had surrounded them on all sides and which threatened to suffocate them. But 'Krishna swallowed the fire, and thus man and beast were saved. The symbol of the forest fire is familiar to the Hindus as the image of the situation of man in this world.... The poor human being sees himself inescapably trapped. The miraculous intervention of Krishna saves him; only when God himself consumes the fire is man saved from being engulfed by it' (Klostermaier, p.23). According to this school of thought it is, indeed, through God's grace alone 'that the *karma* attaching to a soul can be cancelled out and that it can "become Brahman" and through becoming Brahman be in a fit state to draw near to God' (Zaehner, *Hinduism*, p.96). This became the basic tenet of the developed *bhakti* movements.

Buddhism

We get the same double picture in Buddhism. Here too, as in Hinduism, the basic emphasis is on man working out his own salvation – as in the Theravāda doctrine and in Zen Buddhism today. The way of salvation is by a knowledge of the Four Noble Truths, and then by practising the eightfold moral discipline of the 'Middle Way' which is the path to *Nirvāna*.[8] But in the Mahāyāna form of Buddhism, which today is far more widespread, we find a reappearance of the Hindu concept of *avatārs*, among whom Gautama was 'the latest and greatest of a series of eternal Buddhas who had appeared on earth to spread the saving Dharma to suffering humanity'. There are also, as we have seen, 'mythical heroes or Bodhisattva, who, following the example of Gautama, having attained perfect knowledge, refrained from entering

[8] *Cf.* Lewis and Slater, pp.61f. Mention might also be made of the 'four sublime moods'; *cf.* A. L. Basham, *The Wonder that was India*, pp.283f. See also Eliot, Vol. I, pp.213ff.

upon the state of nirvana in order to help mankind by propagating the Dharma of the middle way'. This magnanimous act (involving, as is sometimes believed, the repetition of birth and death as well as the prolongation of the pain and suffering of mundane existence) has had an emotional appeal comparable to that of the gospel – in spite of the fact that the Bodhisattvas were only mythical or legendary figures (*cf.* James, *Christianity and Other Religions,* pp.81f.).

In Pure Land Buddhism, as we have seen, salvation is attained solely by the intervention of Amitābha ('Amida' in Japanese), whose effective help is assured to all who continually invoke his name in prayer – saying, for example,

> Have ye faith in Amida's Vow
> Which takes us in eternally.
> Because of Him, of his Great Grace
> The Light Superb will all be thine.
> (*Shinzu Seiten,* p.236).

Tibetan Lamaism opens the door to another strange world. There are Living Buddhas who can 'conjure up' phantom bodies (largely indistinguishable from ordinary bodies), to help to convert others; reigning Lamas whose 'spiritual principle' can in due course be found 're-incarnated' in the body of a child conceived forty-nine days after his predecessor's death (*cf.* Conze, p.308); *mantras* or magical sayings of great power which can even be inscribed on paper and put in a prayer-wheel; and even Shaktism, in which the worshipper is joined to the universal feminine through directly orgiastic 'worship' (*cf.* Metz, p.237). By contrast, Zen Buddhism concentrates on meditation and severe self-discipline, with no reliance whatever on supernatural aid.

Zoroastrianism

In Zoroastrianism, too, there appears to be an expectation that 'before the end of the world, at intervals of a thousand years each, there will be three saviours. . . . Each will be a supernatural descendent from Zoroaster'. Finally, the last of these, Soshyant, will with his assistants slaughter an ox, and from the fat of the ox 'prepare Hush, and give it to all men. And all men become immortal for ever' (Hume, p.217).

The mystery religions

The concept of a saviour-god was also widespread in Egypt and the Fertile Crescent (*cf.* p.53, above). In Mesopotamia the dominant figure was the goddess Inanna-Ishtar, with her son-spouse, Dumuzi-Tammuz. Each year the young god died and had to be 'rescued and restored' from the land of the dead by Inanna-Ishtar, who resuscitated him and thereby revived life in nature and men. It was she, not he, who was the 'embodiment of creative power in its fullness' and the source of regeneration (*cf.* James, *Christianity and Other Religions,* p.92). In Egypt, on the other hand, the saviour-god was Osiris, lord of the dead, helped and abetted by his sister-wife Isis. It was to Osiris that 'men turned more and more to escape corporeal corruption after death, and to attain a blissful immortality.... This, however, was accomplished by the correct performance of the prescribed ritual techniques whereby Osiris himself had been restored and reanimated by his devoted wife and sister...rather than by justification by faith in the saviour god' (James, *op. cit.,* p.89). And while the appeal of the cult of Isis was primarily to women, it seems to have met the deeper needs of its initiates in a way that no other of the mystery religions did in the pagan world. Yet it failed to make any permanent impression, as E. O. James emphasizes, 'because like the other cults it could not free itself from its underlying mythology. Behind it lay the long history of the religion of ancient Egypt whence it sprang, and though it spread rapidly and assumed increasing importance at the turn of the era, despite its ethical and spiritual elements it could never get away from its ancestry and accretions' (James, *op. cit.,* p.91). In other words, its fundamental weakness was that it rested on religious fantasy rather than historical fact; and this sharply distinguishes it from New Testament Christianity, and the unique historical event – totally unexpected, as it was, by the disciples – which gave birth to the apostolic *kerygma* with which it burst upon the world.

Islam

When we turn to orthodox Islam, we find ourselves confronted by a religion which sprang from a somewhat similar geographical area but which differs from the mystery religions in almost every other respect. It has an unquestionably historical basis, and its central doctrine is a rigid monotheism. It is also pre-eminently a religion of law; and it would be easy to conclude that the attainment of salvation must depend on the quality of obedience to that law which characterizes the life of the individual concerned. But as in other matters, the Muslim community is divided in this respect into a number of different sects. In the view of the Khawārij (who are represented today by the Ibādīs of Oman and North Africa) anyone guilty of a major sin of which he has not repented ceases to be regarded as a believer at all. In the strict doctrine of the Shī'a, on the other hand, a Muslim who dies without recognizing the proper Imām 'dies the death of an unbeliever' – and many Shī'īs not only regard their Imāms as the sole media of divine blessing but attribute to the death of al-Husayn at Karbala something approaching atoning significance. But the clear-cut barriers and distinctions between the different sects of Islam are now breaking down; and I think it would be fair to say that the great majority of Sunnī (or 'orthodox') Muslims, at least, today take the attitude that if they recite the Muslim creed from their hearts, and if they make some attempt to fulfil their obligations in fast and prayer, they may have to taste the fire of judgment for a time but will eventually be 'saved' and admitted to Paradise by the timely intercession of their Prophet. The principle of sacrifice is by no means unknown, as the yearly festival of sacrifice (*al-adhā*) testifies; but it holds no central position in the religion of Islam.

Judaism

In the Judaism of the Old Testament, on the other hand, the sacrificial system clearly held a central place, and the national Day of Atonement became the most important day in the year. But the sacrificial system, as James Atkinson puts it, operated increasingly as time went on by men with a deep awareness of sin, did not mean that by sacrifice a Jew hoped to attain God's grace, but rather that in penitence and faith he sought to retain it and avert its withdrawal. He sought in penitence to recover a favour, a relationship he had once known and had now lost owing to his sin; sin which would earn him wrath and death, if God were not gracious. The whole sacrificial system was an evangelical sacrament of forgiveness and deliverance, and forgiveness and deliverance were entirely God's work, never man's. It was not that man was doing anything to please or propitiate an enigmatic and uncommitted God who had not so far shown his hand. On the contrary, the central element in all Israelite worship was the collective liturgical recollection of all that God had done in their history in visiting and redeeming his people (Atkinson, p.301).

But it seems clear that the sacrificial system of the Old Testament was primarily geared to deal with ceremonial uncleanness and sins committed unwittingly through ignorance, with the purpose of teaching the holiness of God. No specific sacrifices were prescribed for breaches of the Covenant, for arrogant disobedience or for social injustice and oppression. Yet the basic principle that 'without the shedding of blood there is no forgiveness of sins' (Heb. 9:22) must have applied – at least through the Day of Atonement, with its scapegoat and sacrifice. We may perhaps conclude, therefore, that the Law was so framed as to discourage the impression (so vehemently denounced by the prophets) that even the most punctilious observance of ceremonies and abundance of sacrifices could ever take the place of a man's heart repentance and his casting himself on the mercy of God. Paul's deepest sorrow about his fellow-countrymen as a whole was that 'because they did not understand God's righteousness, and sought to establish their own, they did not submit to the righteousness of God' (Rom. 10:3f., C. K. Barrett).

Christianity

But the apostolic teaching about this vital matter was crystal clear. The 'blood of bulls and goats' could never atone for human sin (Heb. 10:4), and the value of the whole sacrificial system – ordained of God as the apostles clearly believed it to be – was twofold: first as an indication and a symbol of that repentance and faith without which, as the Old Testament prophets had passionately proclaimed, no religious observance was of any value whatever; and then as signposts pointing forward to the unique sacrifice of the 'Lamb of God' who was to come, of which all the sin-offerings and Passover lambs were mere foreshadowings. So the Old Testament sacrifices had to be repeated 'year by year' – and even day by day – until in the fullness of time they were 'set aside' by the 'offering of the body of Jesus Christ once for all' (Heb. 10:10). It was, indeed, to this unique historical event of the crucifixion of Jesus that both type and prophecy in the Old Testament – enacted symbol and verbal prediction – had looked forward, and from this event that the Christian church had been born.

But this historical event was not only the fulfilment of the sacrificial system; it was also the basic essential of any fellowship between a holy God and sinful men and women. Such fellowship was impossible without forgiveness; and a holy God, by reason of his very nature, could forgive only on a moral basis. It was not, as in so many religions, that man must try to buy off the vengeance of a malignant God by the sacrifices – animal, human or personal – which he must himself provide, but that God so loved sinful man, and so longed to 'save' him, that he had taken the initiative and 'sent his Son to be the propitiation for our sins' (1 Jn. 4:10). Nor was it that God had accepted the sacrifice of the only man 'good enough to pay the price of sin', for that would be unjust and unthinkable;[9] it was God himself – the God who made us, who put us in this world, and who must have known that we would fall into sin; the God who constitutes

---

[9] *Cf.* Ezk. 18:20, which shows that no man can take the place of another in the matter of sin. Yet it is profoundly true that Jesus died as our representative, and only a man can represent man. It was because he was also God (one with the Father, God-in-manhood) that he could *also* die 'in our place'.

the moral order of the universe, and cannot ignore sin; the God who is the judge before whom we must all stand one day – who was 'in Christ reconciling the world to himself'.[1]

The challenge of Pluralism

So the challenge of Pluralism is not confined to the fact that it puts Jesus substantially on a par with the founders of other religions, or even that it equates the Father of whom he so constantly spoke with the ineffable (but distinctly nebulous) 'Ultimate Reality' to whom (or to which) so many have sought to point. It is, of course, true that there *is* a Transcendent Reality behind all the phenomena of nature and the instinctive questionings of men, and that men and women all over the world, and all down the ages, have reached out after this Mystery – although it would (alas) be going too far to suggest that all the world's great religious leaders have been free from those taints of wishful thinking, idiosyncracy, self-seeking, and liability to deception and error, that afflict us all.

What was unique in Jesus was that he, while genuinely sharing our humanity, could reveal in his own life and person the nature and character of the Father with whom he was essentially one, and could even introduce others into the family and fellowship of God. But to do this involved redemption as well as revelation, the darkness of the cross as well as the mystery of his incarnation and the wonder of his teaching. He alone could truly say 'He who has seen me has seen the Father' and could also speak of 'my blood of the covenant, which is poured out for many for the forgiveness of sins' (Jn. 14:9; Mt. 26:28). This is why, in my experience, although Muslims who have become Christians never suggest that they had not all along been directing their worship to the One, Creator God, they joyfully testify that they now have a very different understanding of his nature and enjoy a wholly new relationship with him.

But this 'salvation' is for the whole world. It would be intolerably arrogant if Christians were to give the impres-

---

[1] This reconciliation, as I have argued elsewhere, involves not only a change in *our* attitude to God and sin, but also an objective atonement which makes it possible for an ever-loving but always holy God righteously to forgive the penitent sinner. See J. N. D. Anderson, *Christianity: the Witness of History*, pp.79ff.

sion that they had anything of themselves to give to others – many of whose ancestors were deeply concerned with the riddle of the universe when ours were sunk in ignorance. What we dare to share is what we have received as a wholly unmerited gift, which the One who gave it to us longs to give them too. Our message is that the *karma* or burden of the past (whether wholly our own, or in part inherited) has been borne by Another, who took our place and 'carried our sins'; and that the reconciliation he died to achieve will ultimately be cosmic in its effects.

It would, of course, be gross injustice for an innocent man to be allowed to suffer in the place of the guilty. Nor would it really do us any good. But what if God himself – our Creator, Sovereign and Judge – were to demonstrate, and put into effect, his eternal plan for our salvation, by giving the 'vulnerability' inherent in his love for us its uttermost manifestation? I myself always come back to Edward Shillito's matchless words:

> The other gods were strong; but Thou wast weak;
> They rode, but Thou didst stumble to a throne;
> But to our wounds only God's wounds can speak,
> And not a god has wounds, but Thou alone.
> *(Jesus of the Scars and Other Poems)*

But they must be *God's* wounds if they are to heal – and this brings us back to the mystery of the incarnation.

To the person of the Saviour, and to the efficacy of the reconciliation he accomplished, God gave unequivocal witness when he raised him from the dead. So the gospel we have to share with others is a 'finished' salvation, to which nothing need be added. It can never be earned or achieved; it can only be accepted by the empty hand of faith. But two points need to be emphasized. First, this faith is no mere mental assent, for it involves a radical change of direction, a basic transfer of allegiance, and a decisive repudiation of both the sin and self-sufficiency of the past. Manifestly, then, it is far from synonymous with 'Christendom', for it is God's way of salvation for the whole world. It was certainly enjoyed by Old Testament Jews who turned to God in repentance and faith (*cf.* Heb.

9:15), little though they understood what God was going to do in Christ, for them and for the world as a whole, in the fullness of time.

What concerns us in this context is Hick's categorical statements that the Christian faith as we know it 'implies that God can be adequately known and responded to *only* through Jesus' and that 'it is by his death alone that men can be saved' (*God Has Many Names*, p.73). Both these statements are, as I see it, absolutely true as they stand; for it seems to me that Acts 4:12 and certain other texts clearly affirm that salvation is to be found in Jesus alone and in what he has done. But Hick is too sweeping, as it seems to me, when he asserts that this necessarily implies that 'the whole religious life of mankind, beyond the stream of Judaic-Christian faith, is thus by implication *excluded as lying outside the sphere of salvation*' (p.73. My italics), and that 'the loving God and Father of all men *has decreed that only those born within one particular thread of human history* shall be saved' (p.74. My italics).

To begin with, he seems to have confused two wholly distinct points in these deductions. The second quotation appears to rest (in part, at least) on the sad fact that the great majority of people in Asia today live and die in the religion into which they were born. But this is certainly not comparably the same in, say, parts of Africa and South America, where the response to the gospel is currently far greater than it is among those born into 'the stream of Judaic-Christian faith'; and which of us knows what God is going to do in the future? And the reply to his first deduction is to affirm that we *dare* not assert that God is not at work by his Spirit, in ways we may not comprehend, among those born in other religious traditions, 'to uproot and tear down, to destroy and overthrow', and then 'to build and to plant' (Je. 1:10) – or, indeed, that he cannot so work in individual lives that they may be brought within the salvation that is in Christ alone, even if they have never been in a position to join his visible church. To this problem we shall revert in chapter 5.

But if Christ is indeed the universal Saviour, then why, it is sometimes asked, could he not have come in person to every race and culture, rather than to one only? To this question there are two basic answers. The first is the vital difference between the concept of an *avatār* and the mystery of the incarnation. In the former, a divine being 'descends' to this world in the bodily form of a man (or some other creature), but without any essential change of nature. To this the nearest biblical equivalent is those 'theophanies' recorded in the Old Testament (*cf*. Gn. 18:1–14; 32:24–30; Jos. 5:13ff.) – and both *avatārs* and theophanies can be repeated indefinitely. In the incarnation, by contrast, we have the almost incredible mystery of God himself, in the person of his 'Son' or 'Word', actually becoming one of us, 'born of a woman', sharing our nature, temptations and experiences, limitations and pain. This was something that is essentially unrepeatable. Almost exactly the same can be said of his death on the cross; for 'Christ, once raised from the dead, is never to die again: he is no longer under the dominion of death' (Rom. 6:9, NEB). Nor is there any need for a repetition of that supreme self-sacrifice by which he 'appeared once for all... to do away with sin' (Heb. 9:26). We now have a 'high priest' who can fully 'sympathize with our weaknesses' (Heb. 4:15) and can 'save for ever' those of every nation 'who come to God through him' (Heb. 7:25). Both the atonement he made, and the reconciliation he affected, was 'once for all' (Heb. 10:10–14).

But is the very idea of God becoming man as incomprehensible, and even 'meaningless', as speaking about 'a square circle'? This, *inter alia*, will be the subject of our next chapter.

4

A unique disclosure?

Introduction

We took as our starting-point in this consideration of Christianity and world religions the proclamation, or *kerygma*, of the apostolic church, since this can be decisively authenticated from the pages of the New Testament. It found its origin and essence in a unique historical event – the life, death and resurrection of someone who had only just died, who had been well known to large numbers of people who were still alive, and whom many of them claimed to have seen after he had risen from the grave; for the apostolic proclamation had no other *raison d'être* or content than these facts and their implications. So our second chapter was devoted to a consideration of this phenomenon of the Christian faith in the light of the origin – whether historical or mythological – of other world religions.

Next, we began to examine in more detail the significance of this historical event as it was understood and proclaimed by the primitive church. Thus our last chapter was concerned with the way in which the apostles – by contrast with other religious teachers – interpreted their message in terms of our human need and longing for 'salvation': that is, deliverance from slavery to sin, self, frustration and fear in this life, and from judgment and loss in the Hereafter – to say nothing of the positive assets of personal 'wholeness', peace with God, and the glorious prospect of a world which will ultimately be set free from all evil, oppression, corruption and decay. So it is now our task to consider the light the Christian revelation sheds on the nature and character of God, and to compare this understanding of the Godhead, and how he can be known to men, with what other religions teach.

There can be no doubt that the apostolic proclamation was firmly rooted in the progressive disclosures of himself which God had given throughout Israel's very chequered history, as these had been recorded in the Old Testament scriptures. In the Acts of the Apostles, Peter, Stephen and Paul all referred to 'the God of our fathers' (Acts 3:13; 7:32; 22:14; *etc.*) and the way in which he had revealed himself to Abraham, Moses, David and the Prophets. Indeed, the teaching of Jesus himself, and of his apostles after him, continually emphasized the fundamental unity, the uncompromising holiness and the changeless love of the God who had, time and again, not only confronted his chosen messengers in existential encounter but had communicated to them words which they must pass on to their contemporaries and which would be recorded for future generations.

It is also clear that, after the resurrection, the first disciples came, at an astonishingly early date, to associate the Jesus they proclaimed with the God of the Old Testament revelation – in a way wholly different from their attitude to Moses or any other figure in their history. They had not yet, it is true, worked out an articulate doctrine of the Trinity – a doctrine, indeed, which would never have emerged from metaphysical speculation but was forced upon them by the impact of personal experience, reflection on what they had seen and heard, and the inward enlightenment of divine disclosure. But they instinctively recognized the essential unity between Jesus and Yahweh, applied to Jesus Old Testament verses which, in origin, clearly applied to Yahweh alone, and felt free – without any qualm of idolatry – to worship Jesus and to address him directly in prayer. As Philip Mason has put it, for example, the author of John's Gospel wanted above all to make it clear that God had not only *seemed* to be a man. He wanted to rub in the astounding fact that the Word, the eternal Word – God in action – really had become flesh – real flesh – flesh and blood and bone; He had walked and talked and His friends had touched Him. But the artist must not obscure the sense of otherness, of Holiness, of Eternal Spirit that they had felt. They had all been in awe of him.... On every page, the contrast, the paradox, is there. His presence in the world was a touch-stone, dividing good from bad. The world was made by Him and the world received Him not. He had overcome the world yet He loved the world (Mason, p.67).

Nor is this attitude by any means confined to John. Take, for example, the very early 'Hymn of the Incarnation' which says of 'Christ Jesus':

Who, being in very nature God, did not consider equality with God something to be grasped, but made himself nothing, taking the very nature of a servant, being made in human likeness. And being found in appearance as a man, he humbled himself and became obedient to death – even death on a cross! Therefore God exalted him to the highest place and gave him the name that is above every name, that at the name of Jesus every knee should bow, in heaven and on earth and under the earth, and every tongue confess that Jesus Christ is Lord, to the glory of God the Father (Phil. 2:6–11).

To this we shall have to return in due course. But first we must pass in brief review the way in which men of other religions have come to understand the Ultimate Reality.

Does religious thought follow an evolutionary pattern?

Not so long ago many anthropologists were content confidently to describe the development of the religious orientation and understanding of mankind in terms of a simple process of evolution of religious thought; for 'evolution' had at that time passed over from being a theory of biology to being regarded as virtually a philosophy of life. Starting

from magic, man had first embraced 'animism',[1] then polytheism and then monotheism – from which, of course,
some would regard atheism as a further stage of progress,
when the age of religion, which had displaced that of
magic, itself gives place to that of science. But this thesis
can no longer be sustained. Religion can scarcely be said to
have 'arisen out of the failure of the magician to exercise his
functions successfully', for in point of fact religion and
magic everywhere 'occur side by side and are inextricably
interwoven'. Indeed, it is not only in pre-literate states of
culture that 'supreme beings, animistic spirits and anima-
tistic conceptions of the sacred and numinous coincide
with magical devices, divination and soothsaying', but
religion and magic are also 'recurrent phenomena in predominantly scientific civilisations'. It is impossible therefore, E. O. James declares, 'to maintain evolutionary
sequences along the lines adopted by Tylor, Frazer and
their contemporaries' (*Christianity and Other Religions*, p.22).

There is, moreover, a great deal of evidence against the
assumption that the development of religion has always
been from polytheism to monotheism. In the contemporary
world, the study of primal religions seems to have established that everywhere – even among the most remote and
primitive tribes – there is a concept of one High or Supreme
God. Thus Stephen Neill insists that there can now be
scarcely any doubt about the existence of such a belief.
'There are', he says,

> still a few unexplored corners of the earth, and no doubt
> there are still surprises awaiting the anthropologists and
> others who interest themselves in simple peoples. But
> the myth that affirmed the existence of tribes which have
> no religion at all has steadily been exploded by the pro-
> gress of research; and some of the most striking evidences
> of a comparatively high level of religious understanding
> have been obtained among the peoples which live on the
> lowest level of subsistence and culture. Thus Fr. W.
> Schmidt (1868–1954), who has given more elaborate study
> to this line of research than any other scholar, found that

[1] The idea (common in primal religions) that physical objects or phenomena have a 'soul',
or are inhabited by some spirit.

115

among the pygmies of Central Africa...there is a clear sense of the existence of one Supreme Being to whom all other existences, natural or supernatural, are subject (Neill, p.131. *Cf*. Schmidt, pp.88, 191f.).

But it is equally clear that this High or Supreme God is given remarkably little thought, prominence or attention in the rites and observances of most primal religions. Instead, men and women are absorbed by the need to propitiate a multitude of far more immanent spirits. 'In many primitive peoples the High God appears to be regarded as a somewhat otiose and functionless being, who after creating the world wandered away into a far region, and so is now no longer very relevant to the practical affairs of life; he is not the object of a cult, nor is sacrifice offered to him' (Farmer, p.44). But the position is far from uniform. A few 'pre-literary societies' (*e.g.* the Ameru of Kenya) are 'practical monotheists'. Even so, 'God does not figure largely in the everyday life of the Ameru. It is the common belief that one should not bother God too much, otherwise he may get angry.' It is he who is the source of good; but 'the ills of everyday life are ascribed either to witchcraft or to the *nkoma* (ancestral shades or 'living dead').... The important thing is to keep them happy and to give them proper respect by performing the correct rituals on death and after death, and by feeding them' (Newing, pp.18f.). Other tribes (*e.g.* the Ashanti) 'have a pantheon of divinities through whom God manifests himself', and their number 'is on the increase' (Mbiti, p.117). There is no trace of a steady progression towards a pure monotheism. On the contrary, it looks as though many tribes have abandoned in practice a monotheism they once knew and still in theory acknowledge, or are stifling an inner conviction which runs counter to beliefs which hold them in fear and bondage.

Thus W. Schmidt himself regards the phenomena as evidence of the survival, in part, of a primitive revelation of God which has become obscured and overladen by magic, animism, polytheism and delusion (Schmidt, p.198). The other interpretation suggested above – which may, indeed, be supplementary rather than contradictory to this – is given by the apostle Paul when he states that men suppress or stifle the truth that they really know.

> For all that may be known of God by men lies plain before their eyes; indeed God himself has disclosed it to them. His invisible attributes, that is to say his ever-lasting power and deity, have been visible, ever since the world began, to the eye of reason, in the things he has made. There is therefore no possible defence for their conduct; knowing God, they have refused to honour him as God, or to render him thanks. Hence all their thinking has ended in futility, and their misguided minds are plunged in darkness. They boast of their wisdom, but they have made fools of themselves, exchanging the splendour of immortal God for an image shaped like mortal man, even for images like birds, beasts, and creeping things (Rom. 1:19–23, NEB).

Nor is this true only of the primal religions. Indeed, Schmidt and his collaborators have shown that a belief in some supreme being is almost universal (Schmidt, pp.251ff.). It can be found in ancient Egypt, Mesopotamia, Iran (James, *Christianity*, pp.51, 53f., 60ff.) and China, for example, but it has in each case been combined with, or overlaid by, polytheistic beliefs and practices. The possibility of some cross-fertilization of ideas between one religion and another cannot, of course, be excluded – to say nothing of the obvious fact that both Buddhism and Jainism sprang from the matrix of Hinduism, and Christianity from that of Judaism. But far from a pattern of evolutionary progress, the evidence for retrogression in religious beliefs and practices in some cases seems at least equally strong. If the import of the Old Testament, for example, is not to be distorted beyond recognition on the basis of preconceived ideas, it seems clear that the religious history of Israel constitutes a unique record of a primitive monotheism which was repeatedly compromised by man's fatal tendency to lapse into superstition, idolatry and unbelief – only to be recalled, temporarily, by yet another summons to return to the God he already knew but so easily forsook, and who never ceased to inspire one prophet after another with what may justly be termed an ever-deepening disclosure of himself.

When we turn to the religions which are extant in the world today we find the most bewildering variety of beliefs on this subject. Of the primal religions little more need be said in this context; but even the most superficial study of Hinduism reveals, as we have seen, that it is made up of very diverse strands and is understood by different people in very different ways. It can scarcely be denied that the popular Hinduism of the masses, for example, represents a form of polytheism (or, at best, a very qualified mono-theism, sometimes termed henotheism[2]) to which expression is given in a variety of idolatrous practices; but the same religion is interpreted by more sophisticated persons sometimes in pantheistic, sometimes in quasi-mono-theistic, and sometimes in impersonal monistic terms. Buddhism, too, takes a number of different and even contradictory forms, whether as a variety of agnostic or atheistic monism, of humanism, of quasi-theism, of an amalgam of two or more religions, or of what has even been termed phantasmagoria (*cf.* pp.63f., 87f., 94–97, above). In Zoroastrianism, again, we find an explicit, if qualified, dualism which constitutes an alternative to either theism or monism in its approach to the problem of evil.[3] But this problem is so intractable, and so basic to our experience, that it will, I think, provide an illuminating approach to the way in which different religions have sought to explain the meaning of human life and the existence, and nature, of the 'Supreme Reality'.

The problem of evil, sin and suffering

In a polytheistic religion this problem finds a comparatively simple solution. There are good gods and bad gods, bene-volent gods and malignant gods, so all depends on which of these different deities is in control at any particular time

[2] Henotheism properly means belief in one God as the deity of the tribe, community or individual without asserting that he is the only God. Loosely, it is sometimes used of those who believe that one supreme God reveals himself through several local or lesser gods.

[3] Zoroastrians believe in two gods or principles of virtually equal power – one good, and the other evil. So all may be said to depend on which is in control in any particular place, time or circumstance.

or place. They are in continual, or at least intermittent, conflict, and neither one nor the other is necessarily destined to prevail. And the picture is not very different when we turn to Hinduism in its popular form. But Hinduism can also be interpreted, as we have seen, as a monotheistic religion, as a form of pantheism, or as an impersonal monism. Those who understand Hinduism in monotheistic terms regard both good and evil as created by, and proceeding directly from, the same God. Thus Klaus Klostermaier, after watching an incident in which a goat died of sunstroke and was immediately torn to pieces first by vultures, then by dogs and finally by jackals, writes:

> God was the creator and preserver and destroyer. The reason for placing creatures in a desert, in a cruel world, in death – that was his caprice, his play, his lila. First he had created the sun who would one day kill the goat he had also created. He had created the vultures who would consume the goat. The dogs and jackals who would tear the skin to pieces and crack the bones with their teeth, they also were his creatures. *One* atman in all of them – in God and in the vulture, in the goat and in the dog. And also in the one who watched all this, trying to understand (Klostermaier, p.77).

It is clear that here an interpretation of Hinduism in terms of a theistic monism or of pure pantheism come very close together. On the one view all that exists, whatever its moral character, proceeds directly from the same God; on the other all that exists constitutes, and is essentially one with, the deity. To those who think in terms of a non-theistic monism, again, there is only one Being – impersonal and absolute – and nothing else has any real existence. The visible world is basically regarded as an illusion or mere appearance (*māyā*) and moral evil as ignorance, or at least as the fruit and evidence of ignorance. At the same time Hindus also believe that certain behaviour will lead to a re-incarnation lower down the scale of life, and thus retard one's hope of ultimately reaching the goal of *moksha* – that is, release from phenomenal existence, with its unceasing transience, rather than from sin, and the attainment (or realization) of unity with the 'One', rather than any form of the beatific vision – except, that is, in the more ardent *bhakti* circles.

In the case of those Hindus who believe in a personal deity, Zaehner writes:

> God originates and sustains the world and reabsorbs it into himself...and his ultimate purpose is the final liberation of all souls from the trammels of matter, which is itself his own 'lower nature'. He binds that he may loose and that he may lead all souls back to himself whether they like it or not. This is the eternal 'game' that he plays with his creation, but like any game it has its own rules, and the rules of the game are called *dharma*. God alone knows the rules, but he can and does on occasion reveal them to man as Krishna[4] did to Arjuna, and man, in his turn, obeys the rules willy-nilly, for he is conditioned by his own *karma* – the works that follow him from lives lived long ago into his present life with the same blind instinct that enables the calf to find the mother-cow wherever she may be in the herd – and by God's own purpose which manifests itself as Fate and Time (*kāla*) and against which it is useless to struggle. Arjuna may not understand with his finite intellect why a fratricidal war involving the slaughter of millions is both necessary and right and therefore part and parcel of 'eternal *dharma*' itself, but loath though he may be to take his cousins' lives he is not in fact a free agent, and must. However wrong the *dharma* imposed on you by your caste and by circumstances may appear to you, you are none the less in duty bound to do it, and if you refuse, then Fate, that is, God's will, will take you by the forelock and make you (*Hinduism*, p.103).

It is only fair at this point to emphasize the distinction that some Hindus have come to make, sometimes in agony of soul, between the *dharma* of their caste, as interpreted by the Brāhmans and even taught by the divine Krishna, and the eternal *dharma* which, in Paul's words, is written on

[4] In one of Vishnu's *avatārs*, in which he instructs Arjuna, a man of the warrior caste, about *dharma*.

men's hearts (Rom. 2:15). It is this *sanātana dharma* that Gandhi and other Hindu reformers have sought to follow. Dr S. Radhakrishnan, for example, has insisted that 'Man is not at the mercy of inexorable fate. If he *wills*, he can improve on his past record. There is no inevitability in history. To assume that we are helpless creatures caught in the current which is sweeping us into the final abyss is to embrace a philosophy of despair, of nihilism' (*Recovery of Faith,* p.4). 'This is fine bracing doctrine', Stephen Neill remarks. But he is clearly dubious about where Dr Radhakrishnan learnt it. 'Did he find it in the Upanishads', he asks, 'or have we here an echo of Carlyle's *Sartor Resartus*?' (Neill, p.86). In any case our immediate concern is not with Hindu reform movements, nor even with the concepts of *karma* and *dharma* as such, but with the revelation of the nature and character of God that can be found in Hindusm – or, indeed, in the Buddhism and Jainism that sprang from the same roots.

The nature of the 'Ultimate Reality'

Jainism, as we have seen, is essentially atheistic, and its metaphysical concepts have considerable affinity with those of the Sāmkhya school of Hindu philosophy (*cf.* Basham, 'Jainism', p.257). Even in the Mahāyāna branch of Buddhism, moreover, while at the supra-mundane level there are 'personal, differentiated forms of the Buddha-essence' (celestial Bodhissattvas, who extend their aid to suffering humanity), at the deepest level ('the body of *dharma* or truth, essence, being') Buddha means 'the impersonal, undifferentiated Absolute or Ultimate' – in a pattern of thought which is remarkably similar in structure to the Advaita Vedānta school of Hinduism (*cf.* pp.59, 90, 101, above). As a very broad generalization about the great Eastern religions, indeed, it could I think be said that while man is intensely concerned with the Ultimate Reality, that Reality – however this may be defined – takes singularly little interest in man. This is poignantly expressed by Carrin Dunne, in an extract from his *Conversations between Buddha and Jesus*, in the course of a talk about a young doctor. I quote:

Jesus: You are right in saying that the only reality is Being. It alone is serious and all the rest is jest. Yes, the young physician will be truly happy if what he loves is Being. His happiness no one can take away. But consider this: suppose it happened that Being itself should fall in love with beings. Suppose Being took beings seriously. What would happen then?

Gotama: You speak of Being as though it were a person, an individuality.

Jesus: The only one, strictly speaking. Who alone is not trapped in selfishness and cut off from reality by concern over his own individuality, since that individuality is Being itself. Being is my Father's secret name (Dunne, in Sebastian Moore, *The Inner Loneliness,* p.34).

We must postpone, for the present, a consideration of the implications of this last sentence in terms of the distinctively Christian revelation of God, and concentrate first on whether the Ultimate Reality is to be conceived of as moral or amoral, involved or aloof, compassionate or impassible. And here there are, I think, at least three possible views. First, to the pantheist, or to the theistic monist such as is described by Klaus Klostermaier in the story of the goat that died of sunstroke (p.119, above), all that exists, whatever its nature, is either an integral part of the Ultimate Reality or proceeds directly from the will and inward working of God.

And much the same, strange to say, is true of what is probably still the dominant school of Islamic scholastic theology, the Ash'ariyya. In al-Ash'ari's view

Man cannot create anything; God is the only creator. Nor does man's power produce any effect on his actions at all. God creates in His creative power (*qudra*) and choice (*ikhtiyār*). Then he creates in him his action corresponding to the power and choice thus created. So the action of the creature is created by God as to initiative and as to production; but it is *acquired* by the creature. By acquisition (*kasb*) is meant that it corresponds to the creature's power and choice, previously created in him, without his having had the slightest effect on the action. He was only the *locus* or subject of the action (Macdonald, p.192).

This means that human evil really proceeds directly from the will and operation of God, although by this doctrine of *kasb* 'al-Ash'arī is supposed to have accounted for free will and entailed responsibility upon men'. But Macdonald immediately adds that it may be doubted whether this really occupied him much, since it 'was open to his God to do good or evil as he chose . . .'.

The view that God is 'aloof' rather than 'involved', on the other hand, may fairly be ascribed, I think, to deists. Their salient characteristic is that, unlike theists, they insist that unaided human reason is perfectly capable of deducing the existence of God from natural phenomena without any need for special revelation. And so it is, for Paul (as we have seen) himself confirms that 'since the creation of the world God's invisible qualities – his eternal power and divine nature – have been clearly seen, being understood from what has been made', so that men who deny this are 'without excuse' (Rom. 1:20). But the inevitable corollary of the deist's view is that a God who creates a world which is to include rational creatures, and is then content to leave these creatures without any communication or special disclosure of himself or his purposes, evinces a singular indifference to their welfare.

On this basis, it is not altogether surprising, then, that one result of men's failure to recognize God's hand even in nature was that they 'lost themselves in mere speculations' (Rom. 1:21, Way's translation). If it is true that in human beings love is a nobler quality than power, then surely this must be true of God too? But it is far from easy to discern the love of God from an unaided contemplation of 'Nature, red in tooth and claw'. The conception of a God 'up there', controlling the universe from outside 'like some almighty, invisible Clockmaker' (to adopt Alan Richardson's vivid phrase), is that of a singularly remote being. And precisely the same is true, *mutatis mutandis*, of those Hindu, Buddhist and Jain schools of thought which think of the Absolute Reality in purely impersonal terms.

Philosophical intrusions

Somewhat different considerations seem to apply to the third possible view, the strange concept of a God who is loving and yet 'impassible', since the concept of divine impassibility seems to have invaded Judaism, Christianity and Islam largely from outside themselves – whether from Greek philosophy or the great Eastern religions. The concept is certainly not indigenous to the Old Testament; it is a complete caricature of the New Testament; and, although it has taken a much firmer hold of Muslim than of Jewish or Christian theology, it cannot be said to emanate from the Qur'ān itself – for the God of the Old Testament, the New Testament and the Qur'ān is essentially a living God, not a cold philosophical abstraction. In the case of Islam Macdonald has diagnosed what happended in vivid terms:

> The Muslim philosophers began, in their innocence, with the following propositions: The Qur'ān is truth and philosophy is truth; but truth can only be one; therefore, the Qur'ān and philosophy must agree. Philosophy they accepted in whole-hearted faith, as it came to them from the Greeks through Egypt and Syria. They took it, not as a mass of more or less contradictory speculation, but as a form of truth. They, in fact, never lost a certain theological attitude. Under such conditions, then, Plato came to them; but it was mostly Plato as interpreted by Porphyrius, that is, as neo-Platonism. Aristotle, too, came to them in the guise of the later Peripatetic schools. But in Aristotle, especially, there entered a perfect knot of entanglement and confusion... parts of the 'Enneads' of Plotinus [translated] into Arabic and entitled 'The Theology of Aristotle'. A more unlucky bit of literary mischief and one more far-reaching in its consequences has never been (Macdonald, pp.162f.).

In the context of our subject, the result has been that the Qur'ānic doctrines of *tanzīh* (the divine transcendence) and *mukhālafa* (the utter difference between God and his creatures) have been so exaggerated as to mean that God is so utterly transcendent that he cannot be affected in any way by his creatures (made glad by their obedience and response, or sad by their disobedience and rejection), on the one hand, and that his designation as 'The Compassionate, the Merciful' may not be interpreted in terms even remotely analogous to human compassion or mercy, on the other.

Happily, there was too much in both the Old and New Testaments that pointed in the opposite direction for Jewish or Christian teaching seriously to embrace such extreme views. All the same, rabbinic, patristic and post-patristic writers were all too apt to think in terms of the Hellenistic concept of an unmoved, unchanging, philosophical abstraction of static perfection rather than the dynamic, living God of the Bible. That God is immutable in his character and unchangingly faithful to his promises is certainly true; but this does not mean that he cannot, and does not, take new initiatives – as in the creation, incarnation, atonement and much else. The Old Testament, again, depicts Yahweh as being 'distressed' and 'afflicted' in the afflictions of his people (Is. 63:9), and grieving over unfaithful Israel as a loving and forgiving husband grieves over an unfaithful wife (*cf*. Hosea, *passim*). Spinoza is wrong when he asserts that 'God is free from passions and is not affected by any emotion of joy and sorrow...strictly speaking, God neither loves nor hates anybody' (*Ethics, I,* 17). On the contrary, his love is not fitful but utterly constant, and his wrath against sin, far from being 'peevish' or irascible, is basically the obverse side of his love.

That there were contacts between Greece and the East in antiquity is well known, and the similarities between Greek and Indian philosophical concepts have often been noted. So there may well have been mutual influences between Hindu, Buddhist and Jain thought on the one side, and Greek philosophy on the other, much earlier than the impact that Neoplatonism made on Jewish, Christian and Muslim thought at a considerably later date. But about this we must not speculate here.

Human self-sufficiency

One point that arises unmistakably from this very brief review of a number of different religions is not so much the

wide variety of sects and schools of thought that seem to
proliferate in each of them, as a fundamental distinction
that spans them all. On the one side, there are those who
believe that men must work out their own salvation –
whether they rely on the ethical quality of their lives or
their services to others, as is common in the West, or, as
one instinctively associates primarily with the East, on a
discipline or system that culminates (or is intended to
culminate) in a subjective experience in which the individual concerned attains a consciousness of his oneness with
nature, with the Ultimate, or with God (as he conceives
him to be).

In recent years a new link has in fact been forged between
the East and West among those whose basic reliance is on
themselves alone, since the West (and particularly America)
has been invaded by propaganda from a variety of different,
yet interrelated systems – Scientology, Est, Life Spring and
other forms of what may loosely be termed 'the human
potential movement'. All these systems, in effect, put on
offer a short-cut to, or substitute for, the older and far more
profound monism of the East, for they claim that men and
women can be brought in an astonishingly short space of
time (but at the cost of a few hundred dollars and a ruthless
process of brain-washing!) to an experiential knowledge of
their inner selves which will release them from their natural
or acquired inhibitions and will ensure social and pro-
fessional success. In some cases, it has been justly
remarked, it 'becomes impossible to say whether a given
movement, trend or school of thought is a secular impulse
that has absorbed Eastern/occult values or an Eastern/
occult teaching that has dressed itself in secular language'
(Alexander, p.2).[5]

This experience, Werner Erhard (the founder of Est, or
'Erhard Seminars Training') asserts, brings the realization
that 'The Self itself is the *ground of all being*, that from which
everything arises... when I get in touch with my self and
you get in touch with your self, we will see the same self'

[5] Brooks Alexander is Editor-in-Chief of *S.C.P. Journal*, produced by the Spiritual Counterfeits Project, Inc., of Berkeley, California. This quotation comes from an editorial article,
entitled 'The Rise of Cosmic Humanism: What is Religion?' in Vol. 5, No. 1, Winter
1981–82, p.2.

(*The Graduate Review*, Nov. 1976, pp.3f.) – or, as he has written elsewhere, that 'Self is all there is. I mean that's it'[6] (*East-West Journal*, Sept. 1974). In other words, the 'human potential movement' concentrates almost exclusively on our subjective experiences, regardless of any objective principles. In effect it substitutes the creature for the Creator, or virtually identifies the two. One senses a harnessing of concepts drawn from Advaita Vedānta Hindu monism, on the one hand, and Zen Buddhism, on the other, in the interests of largely secular (and commercial) advancement; and one inevitably remembers Swami Vivekānanda's statement that 'The Buddhists and the Jains do not depend on God; but the whole force of their religion is directed to the great central truth in every religion: to evolve a God out of man' (*Inspired Talks*, p.218). Behind all this lies the primordial lie with which the serpent persuaded Eve in the garden to eat from the tree of the knowledge of good and evil: 'when you eat of it your eyes will be opened, and you will be like God' (Gn. 3:5). The contrast between this attitude and that of those who take a realistic view of themselves, recognize that their primary need is to be reconciled with God, and accept the fact that they are his workmanship (created in Christ Jesus for purposes, and with potentials, that can be realized only by his guiding hand and through his quickening power) can scarcely be exaggerated.

Human inadequacy

On the other side of this fundamental divide to which I have already referred are those who recognize their need for some 'outside, supernatural aid', but seek this in such a wide variety of different ways. The basic distinction here is between those who are content to seek this aid by means of spiritual truths they believe to be enshrined in some story that is itself frankly mythological, in the treasured remem-

---

[6] The word 'it' here represents 'the unique experience that "*est*" has successfully packaged and marketed as *it*' – namely 'a *direct experience of the self*'. Those who get it 'usually report a euphoric freedom from past encumbrances, the ability to be open, straightforward and honest, an increased ability to assert themselves and a general enthusiasm about life' (Stanley Dokupil and Brooks Alexander, in an article entitled '*Est*: The Philosophy of Self-Worship' in the same issue of *S.C.P. Journal*).

brance of some vivid experience they cannot regard as merely self-generated, or in traditional teaching they have simply accepted on trust, on the one hand, and those who, impelled by an inward conviction of failure, frustration and sin, earnestly seek a revelation of God that truly satisfies the longings of their hearts, the moral demands of their consciences, and the questionings of their minds.

It is in these respects, *inter alia*, that the gospel of Jesus Christ stands alone. The gospel meets the longings of men's hearts in the terms of the New Covenant sealed by his blood: a full and free forgiveness of sins, a personal knowledge of God and an inner transformation of both thoughts and affections. It satisfies the moral demands of their consciences by its revelation of God as not only omnipotent, but also as holy and loving. And it brings assurance to their minds by the sheer weight of the evidence for the fact that God put his seal on the efficacy of Christ's atoning death by raising him from the grave (*cf.* pp.29, 47, above) and exalting him to his right hand as our living Saviour.

The power, holiness and love of God

Tributes to the sovereign omnipotence of the one true God abound in all the great monotheistic religions (as distinct, of course, from polytheism or even Zoroastrian dualism); and the continual references to this attribute may, I think, be said to constitute the salient emphasis of the Qur'ān, and certainly of Islam as a religion. Similar statements can also be found throughout the Old Testament. There, however, we find an almost equal emphasis on the fact that God is holy, while in Islamic teaching the term al-Quddūs (the Holy) is only one of the ninety-nine 'beautiful names' of Allāh.

In the Old Testament most of the references to the 'holiness' of God point *primarily* either to his transcendence over all his creatures (although not in the exaggerated sense of that concept attributed above to the later influence of Greek philosophy) or to the positive gulf between him and the gods of Canaan and other neighbouring countries. The worship of any form of 'image' was expressly forbidden in the Ten Commandments (Ex. 20:3–6); and the prophets repeatedly ridiculed the futility of prayer or worship directed to any man-made 'idol' and denounced the veneration of the 'gods' whom idols were thought to embody or 'project' (*cf.* Ps. 115:4–8; Is. 44:6–20). Even the golden calves declared by Aaron in Exodus 32 and by Jeroboam in 1 Kings 12:28 to represent Yahweh or, more likely, to represent a pedestal over which he was enthroned (Motyer, pp.679f.) were regarded as grave sins, for in the Old Testament the only proper way to envisage the Almighty was by one or other of his descriptive names. It is significant that whenever Israel did resort to material representations or 'projections' of the God of the exodus, it seems to have found it necessary, as we have seen, to borrow some pagan symbol of fertility.

But, whatever may be the sense in which references to the holiness of God most frequently appear in the Old Testament, it is abundantly clear that its understanding of his holiness also included a distinctively moral element – inculcated partly by numerous moral precepts and prohibitions, and partly by elaborate rules about ceremonial 'cleanness' (some of which may have been designed, *inter alia*, to keep Israel isolated from the practices of her neighbours). In addition to the emphasis on both the omnipotence and holiness of God, moreover, the Old Testament includes many moving references to the spontaneous, and often unrequited, love of Yahweh for his covenant people (*cf.* Dt. 7:7f.; Is. 63:9; Je. 31:3; Ho. 3:1).

It is a grave mistake to accept the distinction that is sometimes made between the revelation of God in the Old and New Testaments respectively, for the Bible as a whole represents a progressive, not a contradictory, revelation. Thus in the New Testament, too, we find abundant references to the sovereign omnipotence and holiness of God. The New Testament understanding of the holiness of God, again, includes an insistent emphasis on his demand for an exclusive fidelity and allegiance that – as in the Old Testament – likens every dalliance with any other 'lord' to spiritual adultery (*cf.* 2 Cor. 11:2 with Je. 3:9 and Ezk. 23:37). Paul's attitude to idolatry was, in fact, almost precisely the same as that of the prophets: an idol in itself is

129

'nothing' (1 Cor. 8:4); but behind the actual idols there are 'demons' or false gods, and a Christian 'cannot drink the cup of the Lord and the cup of demons too', or 'have a part in both the Lord's table and the table of demons'.

Paul pertinently asks: 'Are we trying to arouse the Lord's jealousy? Are we stronger than he?' (1 Cor. 10:20ff.). The Christian knows 'that there is no God but one'; yet there are also many 'so-called gods' and 'lords' whom the Christian cannot recognize; so, since 'the sacrifices of pagans are offered to demons, not to God', he must 'flee from idolatry' and any participation in pagan worship (1 Cor. 8:4f.; 10:14, 20). Jesus himself, moreover, told his disciples that they should shun both the ostentatious devotions of Jewish 'hypocrites' and the meaningless 'babbling' of 'pagans' (Mt. 6:5–8). But it is noteworthy that personal holiness is defined in the New Testament exclusively in terms of abstaining from moral sins, rather than ceremonial defilement (*cf.* Mk. 7:18–23; Col. 2:20–23).

Perhaps the most significant verse in the New Testament about the holiness of God – particularly in the context of comparative religion – is 1 John 1:5, which declares that 'God is light and in him is no darkness at all'. The word 'light' is, of course, used in the Bible (as elsewhere) both of illumination and, symbolically, of moral purity; but in this verse there can be no doubt that the second sense is paramount. In our context, therefore, the outstanding significance of this revelation lies in its uniquely Christian attitude to monism and dualism. In sharp distinction from pure monism, from the pantheism and the monistic theism of much Eastern thought, from the virtually unqualified theistic monism of Islam, and even from the misconceptions to which a number of verses in the Bible (if taken in isolation and misconstrued) can, sometimes, give rise, this verse declares categorically that the character of our God consists of utter moral purity and undeviating goodness, in which evil, in any shape or form, has no place whatever. It would be impossible to say of him what Klaus Klostermaier wrote about the gruesome fate of a goat, and his reflections about it all in the light of Hindu thought, in *Hindu and Christian in Vrindaban* (*cf.* p.119, above). Nor, for that matter, could a Christian say of him what Muhammad al-Barqawī wrote of the *irāda*, or will, of Allāh:

> Everything, good or evil, in this world exists by His will.
> He wills the faith of the believer and the piety of the
> religious. If He were to change His will there would be
> neither a true believer nor a pious man. He willeth also
> the unbelief of the unbeliever and the irreligion of the
> wicked and, without that will, there would neither be
> unbelief nor irreligion. All that we do we do by His will;
> what He willeth not does not come to pass (*cf.* Hughes,
> pp. 146f.)

Both these statements include material to which every
Christian would subscribe, but there are other respects in
which they clearly go beyond – and even contradict – the
plain teaching of the Bible.

The fact is that within the monism of 1 John 1:5 there is a
distinct element of Christian dualism. For while the verse
unequivocally declares that God is light, it also acknow-
ledges the reality of 'darkness' and states emphatically that
this has no part in the divine nature – and, at least by
implication, does not proceed directly from the one who is
himself utterly good.

Some perplexing problems

This clearly raises some acute theological problems. God
created all things in Christ, and 'without him nothing was
made that has been made' (Jn. 1:3). Yet evil and sin, suffering and calamities, all exist. Nor is God only Creator. He
is also sovereign Lord, without whose permissive will
nothing can happen. Yet 'this is the message we have heard
from him [whether the immediate reference here is to God
or Christ] . . . that God is light and in him is no darkness at
all' (1 Jn. 1:5). The Bible, from cover to cover, makes it clear
that God hates sin and commands men not to sin; yet sin
they do. We are explicitly told that God 'wants all men to be
saved and to come to a knowledge of the truth' (1 Tim. 2:4)
and that he is very patient with us, 'not wanting anyone to
perish, but everyone to come to repentance' (2 Pet. 3:9); yet
by no means 'everyone' does repent or 'come to a knowledge

131

of the truth' – and while some are saved, others perish.
There is a vast difference between the ring of these quotations from the New Testament – or, indeed, in the statement
of Jesus himself (after telling the parable of the Lost Sheep)
that our 'Father in heaven is not willing that any of these
little ones should be lost' (Mt. 18:14) – and the words in the
Articles of Belief of Najm al-Dīn al-Nasafī (a great Muslim
theologian):

> God Most High is the Creator of all actions of His
> creatures, whether of unbelief or belief, of obedience or
> of rebellion; all of them are by the will of God and His
> sentence and His conclusion and His decreeing
> (Macdonald, p.310).

When we turn to the Bible, neither the Old nor the New
Testament gives any full explanation of the searing mystery
of evil, sin, calamity and suffering. As we have seen, the
character of God is completely devoid of evil; yet evil
persists. God is omnipotent, and could – and one day will –
eliminate all that is foreign to his nature. For the present,
however, evil in all its forms is still very much with us. Any
explanation, therefore, must start from the obvious fact
that God has given some of his creatures a considerable
degree of freedom of choice, including the power to act in
ways which are contrary to his revealed will – and even
their own consciences. Satan and all that is demonic were
created by God, but are temporarily permitted to defy him;
and the same applies to his human creatures.

Clearly then, if I may so put it, God must have known
that his ultimate purpose for the world and for mankind
could best – perhaps only – be accomplished in this way.
Only so, it would seem, could he bring 'many sons' to the
glory of a genuinely filial relationship to him now, based
on a conscious moral choice, and ultimately liberate
'creation itself from its bondage to decay' and bring it 'into
the glorious freedom of the children of God' (Rom. 8:21). It
must be that the final end will be so wonderful as to out-
weigh all the intervening 'groaning', frustration and suffering. Meanwhile, God is still sovereign. He has in no
sense lost control of his creation; his purposes both will be,

and are being, fulfilled; and he can and does overrule even sin, disobedience and all that is contrary to his nature for the fulfilment of these purposes (*cf.* Gn. 45:4–8; Acts 2:23).

It is much the same in regard to calamities and disease. The Bible makes it clear that calamities sometimes represent the judgment of God on the individuals concerned, and that suffering sometimes comes directly from his hand as punishment, warning or discipline. But not always so, by any means; for it was Jesus himself who said that 'the Galileans whose blood Pilate had mixed with their sacrifices', and 'those eighteen who died when the tower in Siloam fell on them', were 'no more guilty than all the others living in Jerusalem', and then warned his questioners: 'But unless you repent, you too will all perish' (Lk. 13:1–5). When, moreover, his disciples asked him whether a man whose congenital blindness he healed had been born blind because of his own or his parents' sin, he replied: 'Neither this man nor his parents sinned, but this happened so that the work of God might be displayed in his life' (Jn. 9:3). And although much could be said, by way of exegesis or speculation, about all these problems, the fact remains that neither the book of Job, nor even Jesus himself, has given us any full explanation of them – although it is transparently clear that neither the Old nor the New Testament attributes calamities or misfortunes to anything resembling the Hindu or Buddhist concept of *karma*.

Light in the darkness

In one sense it can be said that we have to take all this on trust – trust in the character of God. But it is precisely at this point that the unique element in the gospel message intervenes for our assurance, and gives us the key to the mystery of suffering, if not any full explanation. For in the incarnation God himself became man in Jesus, who was 'born of a woman', lived a truly human life and died an agonizing human death. As the prophet foretold, he was a 'man of sorrows, and familiar with suffering' (Is. 53:3); he was 'made like his brethren in every respect' (Heb. 2:17); he was 'tempted in every way, just as we are – yet without sinning' (Heb. 4:15); he 'learned obedience in the school of

133

suffering' (Heb. 5:8, NEB); and while his prayers were normally tranquil conversations with 'Abba' (my own Father), he knew, on two occasions at least, what it was to 'offer up prayers and petitions with loud cries and tears' (Heb. 5:7). This means that he really did 'share [our] humanity' (Heb. 2:14) and that Docetism (which, in its extreme form, divinizes even his humanity) is contrary to the New Testament revelation. But had he not also been God (although genuinely 'made man' in and through the eternal 'Son' or 'Word', who is of 'one substance with the Father' in the unity of the triune Godhead), then all this would avail us nothing, except as a magnificent example. It would then not be true to assert that the God who made us and put us in this world, with its mystery of temptation and suffering, had himself shared it all; that 'God was reconciling the world to himself in Christ, not counting men's sins against them' (2 Cor. 5:19); and that in the ascended and exalted Christ we have a glorified man on the throne of the universe.

But how could God become man – not a hybrid 'God-man', but rather 'God-in-manhood' (giving a full meaning to both words)? Frankly I am not impressed by the arguments of those who say that to talk about God becoming man is as 'meaningless' as to talk about a 'square circle', or who insist that the ontology of 'the eternal God and a historical man' are so utterly different that 'it is simply unintelligible to declare them identical'. The fact is that we do know what both a square and a circle are, and that the one is contradictory to the other. But it would be exceedingly bold to claim that we really know the nature of man – or, still more, of man as God designed him to be; and it would be lunacy to suggest that we really know the nature of God. There is, of course, a vast difference between the ontology of the eternal God and that of a historical man; but Christians all down the ages have believed that the nature of our God is such that he could, and did (in the unique mystery of the incarnation), reveal himself once in the ontology of one particular man. Unlike the 'brute beasts', man was originally created in the image and likeness of God, a moral and rational being; but he fell into sin, and that 'image' was marred – and can now be seen only in the one who was, and is, 'the express image of his person' (Heb. 1:3, AV). So, as Brian Hebblethwaite has aptly put it, 'who are we to say that the ontological status of God is such as to render [the incarnation] logically impossible?' (Hebblethwaite, pp.85f.; Anderson, *The Mystery of the Incarnation*, pp.94f.). We must approach this mystery by weighing all the available evidence, rather than dismiss it out of hand as an impossibility on the basis of some philosophical syllogism. And the evidence seems to me singularly convincing.

It is directly contrary to that evidence to suggest that, after the resurrection, the apostolic church embarked on a gradual, and largely unconscious, process of 'deifying' Jesus (*cf. The Myth of God Incarnate*). The evidence is that, almost at once, the church felt at liberty to invoke Jesus in prayer, to worship him, to apply to him Old Testament verses which, in origin, clearly referred to Yahweh himself, and to call him 'Lord' – in the sense in which the Septuagint uses this term to translate the Hebrew *Adonai* as a substitute for the 'unspeakable' name of Israel's covenant God. As we have seen, moreover, it was only a few years before Paul the Pharisee wrote to the Thessalonians reminding them how they had 'turned to God from idols to serve the living and true God, and to wait for his Son from heaven, whom he raised from the dead – Jesus, who rescues us from the coming wrath' (1 Thes. 1:9f.).

Naturally enough, therefore, Jewish Christians were challenged as to whether they were, in fact, still monotheists. This largely explains why the major controversies in the church about the nature of the triune God preceded those about Christology as such; and why the latter were more concerned with deductive arguments 'from above' (that is, from the Trinity to Jesus of Nazareth) than inductive arguments 'from below' (that is, from the New Testament revelation about Jesus to the triune God). But the fact is that, after the resurrection, the apostles found themselves quite naturally associating – and, in some sense, identifying – Jesus with God. This was not the result of metaphysical reasoning, and they certainly had not worked out any formal doctrine of the Trinity. They came to their faith, as was right and proper, on the basis of both revelation and experience – by which, alone, God can really be known. So the earliest Christian creed was 'Jesus is Lord' – Lord, that is, of the whole world. He is not one of many roads to God, but 'the way and the truth and the life' (which may well be a Hebraic way of saying that he is 'the true and living way'). And if Jesus was the revelation of God in terms of a human life, then it follows that God himself is both 'light' and 'love'.

5

No other name?

In our second chapter we started from the *kerygma* of the apostolic church and the unique historical event which gave it birth. We saw, first, how this draws a sharp line of distinction between the Christian faith and all those religions which have a mythological origin, or which basically consist in theological or ethical concepts that are essentially independent of the persons, historical or otherwise, to whom they are officially attributed. Equally, it distinguishes Christianity from those religions which look back to some historical event that had a profound, but essentially different, significance.[1]

In our third chapter we examined the impact and meaning of this unique historical event from the point of view of Christian experience and compared it with the idea of 'salvation' in other religions and ideologies – whether in terms of this world or of life beyond the grave. We saw that there are, indeed, parallels to some aspects of Christian doctrine in a number of different religions, but that the core and essence of the Christian faith is *sui generis*, for it is directly derived from, and essentially dependent on, the unique event to which it always looks back. And in our last chapter we considered that event once more, this time from the point of view of the light it throws on the nature of God –

---

[1] *E.g.* Gautama's Enlightenment under the Bo-tree, Muhammad's Hijra from Mecca, and even Israel's exodus from Egypt – although the last is, of course, part of the Christian heritage, and prefigures our redemption in Christ Jesus.

partly in the context of the baffling, and agonizing, problem of evil, and partly in that of the self-disclosure of God which it essentially provides.

The 'scandal of particularity'

In each of these chapters we described as 'unique' both the historical event from which we started (and, indeed, from which the Christian faith itself arose) and the salvation and disclosure of the Godhead which flow from it. This was not, of course, intended for a moment to suggest that God has revealed himself in no other way and at no other time. Any such idea would be decisively refuted by the self-disclosure of God in the history of Israel and in the Old Testament scriptures – and it will be our duty, *inter alia*, in this present chapter to consider what view we should take of the claim that God has in part revealed himself in many different ways (*e.g.* in nature and conscience), and that there is some truth in almost all the world's religions. The term 'unique' is intended to signify that the historical event on which Christianity is founded is itself without parallel, as is also – in its fullness and essential nature – the salvation which it offers and the self-disclosure of God which it enshrines.

This can, I think, be summed up by two quotations. As Edwyn Bevan puts it:

> the great dividing line is that which marks off all those who hold that the relation of Jesus to God – however they describe or formulate it – is of such a kind that it could not be repeated in any other individual – that to speak, in fact, of its being repeated in one *other* individual is a contradiction in terms, since any individual standing in that relation to God would *be* Jesus, and that Jesus, in virtue of this relation, has the same absolute claim upon all men's worship and loyalty as belongs to God. A persuasion of this sort of uniqueness attaching to Jesus seems to me the essential characteristic of what has actually in the field of human history been Christianity (Bevan, *Hellenism and Christianity*, p.271).

Similarly, E. O. James asserts that

> the Godhead attributed to the founder of Christianity, alike in the New Testament and by the Church, renders it unique in the history of religion. Nowhere else had it ever been claimed that a historical founder of any religion was the one and only supreme deity (James, *Christianity*, p.170).

The New Testament is emphatic, moreover, that God's self-disclosure in Jesus was 'once for all'. Teaching may, indeed, be repeated many times, as may also God's verbal messages to man. But his supreme Message, in a life that was lived and a death that was died, can never be repeated or reproduced.

Inevitably, this is a doctrine which provokes opposition. Paul himself was under no illusions about this; for he tells us that in his day the 'preaching of the cross' was to the Jews a scandal and to the Greeks an absurdity (1 Cor. 1:23). Nor is it only the content of the Christian proclamation which men and women, left to themselves, find unacceptable; still more, perhaps, in this exceedingly tolerant age, it is its exclusiveness and apparent intolerance which stick in men's throats. In many circles today almost any teaching will be accepted as at least a possible contribution to the truth provided only that it does not imply any denial of the validity of other contributions – however mutually incompatible these different contributions may be. As Francis Schaeffer insists, the logic of thesis and antithesis has been abandoned in favour of a comprehensive, but wholly illogical, synthesis (Schaeffer, p.41).

But in this matter synthesis is not a viable option. It is, of course, a common experience for a Christian to learn much from men of other faiths – in devotion, humility, courage and a host of other virtues; and it is perfectly possible for him to learn from his contact and dialogue with non-Christians truths he had not apprehended before. But this is a very different matter from the sort of synthesis which aspires to construct a syncretic religion. In short, the Christian answer, as I see it, must always be: 'Dialogue, yes; syncretism, no.' For if God could have *adequately* revealed himself in any other way, how can one possibly believe he would have gone to the almost unbelievable length of the incarnation? This was no mere theophany, we must remind ourselves; no mere appearance of God among men, as a Hindu believes to have happened in an *avatār*. It was God actually *becoming* man, with all that this necessarily involved. And if God could have dealt with the problem of evil in any other way whatever, how can one possibly believe that he would, in Christ, himself have taken the sinner's place and borne the sinner's guilt – with all the agony (to say nothing of the mystery) expressed in that cry of dereliction from the cross: 'My God, my God, why hast thou forsaken me?' (Mk. 15:34).

Inevitably, then, the Christian faith is either itself false or 'casts the shadow of falsehood, or at least of imperfect truth, on every other system. This Christian claim', as Stephen Neill insists,

> is naturally offensive to the adherents of every other religious system. It is almost as offensive to modern man, brought up in the atmosphere of relativism, in which tolerance is regarded almost as the highest of the virtues. But we must not suppose that this claim to universal validity is something that can quietly be removed from the Gospel without changing it into something entirely different from what it is. The mission of Jesus was limited to the Jews and did not look immediately beyond them; but his life, his method and his message do not make sense, unless they are interpreted in the light of his own conviction that he was in fact the final and decisive word of God to men ... For the human sickness there is one specific remedy, and this is it. There is no other (Neill, pp. 16f.).

This seems to me to be the clear import of the teaching of the Bible. There are a number of relevant verses which demand consideration in this context. But some, I think, are more fundamental than others.

Some sayings of Jesus

One verse which used to be cited in this connection is John 10:8, where Jesus is quoted as having said: 'All who came before me are thieves and robbers; but the sheep did not heed them.' At first sight this would certainly appear to be a singularly sweeping and categorical statement, which might be thought to include in its condemnation all previous religious teachers without exception. But it clearly cannot, in fact, have any such far-ranging import, for it is unthinkable that Jesus should have included Abraham, Moses, David or John the Baptist, for example – to all of whom he bore witness elsewhere as having actually testified of him – in such a denunciation. The words must be governed by the definition of 'a thief and a robber' given just before: namely, 'he who does not enter the sheepfold by the door but climbs in by another way' (Jn. 10:1) – and this *could* in theory, I suppose, refer to all those who had made false Messianic claims or bogus pretensions to being 'saviours'. But this particular discourse can best be understood in the light of the controversy with some of the Pharisees which immediately precedes it. It is almost certain that Jesus must have had the false shepherds of Ezekiel 34 in mind; and there the denunciation is clearly addressed to unfaithful Jewish rulers. As R. H. Lightfoot puts it:

> It is a basic tenet of this gospel that the true leaders of Israel, from Abraham and Moses to John the Baptist, looked forward to the coming of the Lord and bore witness to Him; hence there is obviously no reference in this verse to them...Rather, the verse is a very strong expression, in negative form, of the fact that all truth is now present in the incarnate Lord (R. H. Lightfoot, p.210).

It is unlikely, then, that the founders and teachers of other religions were in fact within the meaning and intention of these words. The phrase 'thieves and robbers' clearly implies an intention to take – whether by stealth or force – what belongs to another, so it would scarcely be applicable to one who, in all sincerity, gave teaching which he thought (however mistakenly) to be true; but it *could* certainly apply to one who claimed to be a saviour when in fact he knew he was not. Yet it is significant that W. Hendriksen considers it unrealistic to think here even of false Messiahs who had arisen before the beginning of Christ's ministry. The context, he asserts,

> says nothing about them. Without any question, it would seem to us, Jesus is thinking here of the men who are standing right in front of him as he is speaking, namely, the religious leaders of the people, the members of the Sanhedrin, Sadducees and Pharisees, but especially the latter (see 9:40; 10:19). *They* were the ones who were trying, by means of intimidation (9:22), to steal the people, and thus to gain honour for themselves in an illegitimate manner. If threats were insufficient, they would use violence. They were, indeed, both thieves and robbers. Moreover, they were already on the scene when Jesus came into the world . . . Hence, it is easy to understand why Jesus says that they had come *before* him. It is also understandable that Jesus says, '*are* (not *were*) thieves and robbers.' They had not disappeared, but were still present (Hendriksen, pp.108f.).

It is also noteworthy that this verse ends with the explicit assertion that 'the sheep did not heed' these thieves and robbers, which would appear to limit the import of the denunciation to false teachers among the Jews.

Considerably more central to our subject are the words in John 14:6: 'I am the way, and the truth, and the life; no one comes to the Father, but by me.' Here the import of the first half of the verse is clear enough: it constitutes an unequivocal affirmation that in the incarnate Lord, uniquely, men can find the road to God, the truth about God, and the life of God. It is the utterly exclusive claim of the second part of the verse which gives us pause: that there is no other way whatever. And with this we may couple the categorical statement in the synoptic tradition that 'no one knows the Father except the Son and any one to whom the Son chooses to reveal him' (Mt. 11:27), and also the stern warning in 1 John 2:23: 'No one who denies the Son has the Father. He who confesses the Son has the Father also.' It may well be that J. A. T. Robinson was right when he suggested that 'the primary purpose of John's Gospel was to lead the Jews of the Dispersion to faith in Jesus as the Christ, the Son of God, while that of the Epistles of John was to warn Jews of the Dispersion who had already come to faith in Christ against the tragedy of falling into apostasy (*Twelve New Testament Studies,* pp. 107–138). But while this might explain the emphasis on the element of denial in the last of these verses, it can scarcely alter the import of the exclusive claim which is common to them all.

Taken by themselves, the thrust of these verses might conceivably be softened by the argument that what they basically assert is that no-one can come to know God *as Father* except through Christ the Son, rather than that no-one can come to know God at all except through him. In point of fact, however, they do not stand alone, but must be read in conjunction with the apostolic proclamation in Acts 4:12 that 'there is salvation in no one else, for there is no other name under heaven given among men by which we must be saved'. It is, of course, perfectly in order to observe that in the Bible the 'name' of God or Christ is often used as a synonym for his revealed character; but I cannot see that this makes any significant difference in this context. It seems to me that the consistent teaching of these verses as a whole – indeed, their necessary and inescapable import – is that it is *only* through Christ that any man can come to a personal knowledge of (and fellowship with) God, and *only* through his life, death and resurrection that any man can come to an experience of salvation. To quote Stephen Neill once more: 'For the human sickness there is one specific remedy, and this is it. There is no other.'

The pre-Christian era

But the question immediately arises as to how, precisely, this applies to those who came before Christ – to Abraham, Moses, David and John the Baptist, for instance. And if it is answered that each of these came to know God, and to enjoy his forgiveness and fellowship, through the Christ whose coming they in part discerned and to whom they all bore testimony, then what of the multitude of repentant and believing Jews who can scarcely be thought to have had any such vivid spiritual perception of what God was going to do in the future? Here, as it seems to me, there can be only one answer: that when an Israelite came to realize that he was a sinner, when he turned to God in repentance and faith, and when he brought his sin offering (where this was required), he was in fact accepted and forgiven – *not* on the basis of the animal sacrifice he had brought, but on the basis of what that sacrifice foreshadowed. The Old Testament sacrifices pointed forward to what God himself did in Christ, the Lamb of God, when he died on the cross for sinful men. That David, for example, did enjoy this forgiveness as a conscious experience Paul clearly teaches (Rom. 4:7f.), and this is palpably apparent in the Psalms he wrote; and animal sacrifices could never take away human sins. Indeed, an essential element in the propitiation Christ made on the cross was, the apostle tells us, that God meant by this 'to demonstrate his justice, because in his forbearance he had overlooked the sins of the past' (Rom. 3:25; *cf.* Heb. 9:15) – for the moral basis on which forgiveness was always available was the redemption finally effected in Christ.

It seems clear, then, that believing Jews under the Old Testament dispensation enjoyed forgiveness and salvation through that saving work of God in Christ (dated, of course, according to the calendars of men, but timeless and eternal in its divine significance), by which alone a holy God can and does forgive the repentant sinner – little though most of them can have understood this.

What, then, was the difference between the experience of believers in Old Testament times and that of Christians under the New Covenant? It was not that devout Jews were saved by 'works' or by their obedience to the law; for no-one can ever be saved by 'works', and no Jew has ever succeeded in keeping the law (Rom. 3:19; Gal. 3:21f.). Believers under the Old Covenant were saved by grace through faith, just as we are: that is, through the grace of God in Christ. But they (if I may here deliberately, but perhaps excusably, misquote Scripture) saw 'in a mirror dimly' (or, as the NEB puts it, 'puzzling reflections in a mirror'), while we, comparatively speaking, already see 'face to face' (1 Cor. 13:12). Under the Old Covenant they had 'but a shadow, and no true image, of the good things which were to come', and had to offer 'the same sacrifices year after year' which could 'never bring the worshippers to perfection' (Heb. 10:1, NEB), while we rejoice in 'the offering of the body of Jesus Christ once for all' (Heb. 10:10), and a forgiveness which excludes any further offering for sin and brings assurance to both heart and conscience. Their knowledge was deficient, their assurance often fitful, but their forgiven status identical with ours. But how ashamed we should be when we compare the poverty of our own actual experience of God with that of Enoch, Abraham, David or Daniel.

This reminds us that the knowledge of God and the experience of his grace were never limited to Israel under the covenant of Sinai. God had called Abram, and subsequently made a covenant with him, hundreds of years before that of Sinai (Gal. 3:17); and under this covenant of 'grace through faith' not only Isaac, Jacob and Joseph lived, but also, for example, Abraham's servant (Gn. 24:52). It is significant that among those 'commended for their faith' in Hebrews 11 we find the names of Abel, Enoch, Noah and Rahab. As Tasker puts it: 'Faith is a practical response to the divine initiative.' So, 'in order to show that it is universally applicable and allows of no exceptions', James 'cites the case of one who was a Gentile, a woman, and a prostitute' (Tasker, pp.70f.). The mysterious Melchizedek, moreover, was both King of Salem (probably Jerusalem) and priest of 'God Most High', in whose name he blessed Abram; and the Massoretic text, by adding 'Yahweh' before 'God Most High' in the oath that Abram then swore to the king of Sodom (Gn. 14:22), emphasizes 'that the two names denote one and the same God' (Bruce, *IBD*, p.977).

Those today who have never heard the gospel

So far, then, the teaching of the Bible seems clear enough. But there remain a number of difficult problems with which we must attempt to grapple. And the first and most perplexing, which must inevitably occur to each of us at this point, is simply this: if the only way to God is through

Christ, and the only basis of forgiveness and acceptance is the atonement effected at the cross, then what about all those countless millions of people in the world today – to say nothing of the millions who have already lived and died – who, to our shame, have never heard of the only Mediator and only Saviour? Are they utterly without hope, as many of our missionary forebears firmly believed? That would be an agonizing thought – which did, to be sure, spur them on to much sacrificial witness, as it still does many today.

Others insist that those who have never heard the gospel will be judged, and may in some cases be justified, by reference to the 'light' that was in fact available to them. It is true, no doubt, that it is by this standard that the quality of their lives will be judged; for we have Paul's authority for the premise that, whereas the Jew will be judged on the basis of the Law revealed on Sinai, non-Jews will be judged according to the criterion of the requirements of the law 'written on their hearts' (Rom. 2:14ff.). The most elementary principles of justice would, indeed, seem to demand this; but I cannot see that it provides any sort of solution to our problem. For the fact remains that, just as no Jew has ever succeeded in keeping the Mosaic Law or the injunctions of the prophets, so no non-Jew has ever succeeded in living up to the standard of the moral and ethical principles according to which he knows that he ought to regulate his conduct. We only need to turn from the second to the third chapter of the Epistle to the Romans to read that 'no human being can be justified in the sight of God' on the basis of law, whatever that law may be, for 'law brings only the consciousness of sin' (Rom. 3:20, NEB). To this there can be no exception. The verdict of God is explicit and unequivocal: 'all have sinned and fall short of the glory of God' (Rom. 3:23).

So our problem comes down to this: is there any basis on which the efficacy of the one atonement can avail those who have never heard about it? It is not enough to say, with Wilfred Cantwell Smith, that 'a Buddhist who is saved, or a Hindu or Muslim or whoever, is saved, and is saved only, because God is the kind of God whom Jesus Christ has revealed Him to be' (*The Faith of Other Men*, p.126). This is clearly true, so far as it goes – for the character and nature of the God with whom we have to do is fundamental. But his character, as revealed in the Bible (and, indeed, in Christ himself), does not solely and only consist in a profound and universal benevolence. God is 'light' as well as 'love', 'justice' as well as 'mercy', and to concentrate on the one quality alone is not only to distort his character but to caricature the essence of his love. As we have seen, God's hatred of sin is, in reality, the inevitable concomitant of his love for the sinner: the reverse side of the very same coin. Inevitably, sin separates from God. It is gloriously true that God 'desires all men to be saved and to come to the knowledge of the truth' (1 Tim. 2:4), but this can be only through the Saviour who is himself 'the propitiation for our sins, and not for ours only but also for the sins of the whole world' (1 Jn. 2:2).

So again we come back to the same question: how can this come about if they have never heard of the only Saviour? But we must, at this point, take to heart Lesslie Newbigin's pungent response to Hans Küng's criticism[2] of Protestant theologians' escape into agnosticism on this subject:

I find it astonishing that a theologian should think he has the authority to inform us in advance who is going to be 'saved' on the last day. It is not accidental that these ecclesiastical announcements are always moralistic in tone: it is the 'men of good will,' the 'sincere' followers of other religions, the 'observers of the law' who are informed in advance that their seats in heaven are securely booked. This is the exact opposite of the teaching of the New Testament. Here emphasis is always on surprise. It is the sinners who will be welcomed and those who were confident that their place was secure who will find themselves outside. God will shock the righteous by his limitless generosity and by his tremendous severity. The ragged beggars from the lanes and ditches will be in the festal hall, and the man who thought his own clothes were good enough will find himself thrown out (Matt. 22:1–14). The honest, hard-working lad will be out in the dark while the young scoundrel is having a party in his father's house (Luke 15). The branch that was part of the

---

[2]*Cf. On Being a Christian*, p.99.

vine will be cut off and burned (John 15). There will be astonishment both among the saved and among the lost (Matt. 25:31–46). And so we are warned to judge nothing before the time (1 Cor. 4:1–5). To refuse to answer the question which our Lord himself refused to answer (Luke 13:23–30) is not 'supercilious'; it is simply honest (*The Open Secret*, p.196).

Many Protestant theologians, indeed, believe that we must leave at this point the question of the eternal destiny of all those who have never heard the gospel, since the Bible does not seem to provide any explicit solution to this problem. Others, I know, insist that various references in the New Testament to saving faith seem to confine this to explicit faith in the Lord Jesus Christ. This is no doubt true; but we are concerned not only with faith but also with grace (*e.g.* the problem of those who die in infancy). So in the next few pages I shall venture to suggest an approach to this whole problem which has increasingly commended itself to me in recent years as one which is compatible with our biblical data – although I realize, of course, that many scholarly and devout people will not agree. I shall then return to the rather different question which, as Newbigin rightly says, 'our Lord refused to answer'.

My suggestion is that we can, perhaps, find a ray of light by going back to what we have already said about those multitudes of Jews who, in Old Testament times, turned to God in repentance, brought the prescribed sacrifice (where such was provided) and threw themselves on his mercy. It was not that they *earned* that mercy by their repentance or obedience, or that an animal sacrifice could ever avail to atone for human sin. It was that their repentance and faith (themselves, of course, the result of God's work in their hearts) opened the gate, as it were, to the grace, mercy and forgiveness which he always longed to extend to them, and which was to be made for ever available at the cross on which Christ 'gave himself a ransom for all, to be testified in due time' (1 Tim.2:6, AV). It is true that they had a special divine revelation in which to put their trust. But might it not be true of the follower of some other religion that the God of all mercy had worked in his heart by his Spirit, bringing him in some measure to realize his sin and need for forgiveness, and enabling him, in the twilight as it were, to throw himself on God's mercy?

Romans 10:12–18

One of the most explicit passages in the New Testament on this subject is Romans 10:12–18. Here Paul makes the unequivocal statement that 'there is no difference between Jew and Gentile – the same Lord is Lord of all and richly blesses all who call on him, for, "Everyone who calls on the name of the Lord will be saved."' On this Calvin comments:

> If the One who is the Creator and Maker of the whole world is the God of all mankind, He will display His kindness to all by whom He has been invoked.... Since His mercy is infinite, it must necessarily extend to all who have sought it.... It follows that the grace of God penetrates to the very abyss of death, if only men seek it from there, so that it is by no means to be withheld from the Gentiles (*Romans*, p.229).

Then, in verses 14 and 15, the apostle insists that the gospel must be proclaimed to the whole world by those whom God sends as his heralds. This was, indeed, the conviction which inspired and sustained Paul's own insistent evangelism, and should sustain ours. But it is important to note that 'To understand this rhetorical climax', as Calvin puts it, 'we must first bear in mind that there was a mutual connexion between the calling of the Gentiles and the ministry which Paul exercised among them, so that the esteem in which the one was held depended on the approbation accorded to the other' (*Romans*, p.229). He also insists that

> it is the preached Word alone which Paul has here described, for this is the normal mode which the Lord has appointed for imparting His Word. If it is contended from this that God can instil a knowledge of Himself among men only by means of preaching, we shall deny that this was the meaning of the apostle. Paul was refer-

ring only to the ordinary dispensation of God, and had no desire to prescribe a law to His grace (*Romans,* p.231).

Calvin does not specify in what ways (other than preaching the gospel) God may sometimes, in his grace, 'instil a knowledge of Himself'; and I certainly do not claim his authority for my own suggestions. We cannot doubt, however, that God can – and sometimes does – communicate directly with individuals. The Old Testament records many occasions when God 'moved' men's hearts (*e.g.* Cyrus) or spoke to them – whether for their own good or that of others – through dreams (*e.g.* Abimelech, Joseph and Nebuchadnezzar), miracles (*e.g.* Naaman), visions (*e.g.* Belshazzar) or in some unspecified way (*e.g.* Balaam).[3] On occasion he spoke, or revealed himself, through a theophany (*e.g.* Jacob and Joshua) or through angels (*e.g.* Hagar and Lot);[4] and both Abram the Aramaean and Saul the Pharisee were the recipients of a number of different revelations, by speech (audible or inaudible), visions and dreams.[5] He has also always made himself known – whether for condemnation or salvation – through the phenomena of nature (*cf.* Rom. 1:19f.; 10:18f.).

It is in this context, to quote Calvin once more, that the apostle

> asks the question whether God had ever before directed His Voice to the Gentiles, and performed the office of Teacher to the whole world. For the purpose of showing that the school into which God might gather scholars to Himself from every part of the world is open to all, he also cites the testimony of the psalmist from Ps. 19:4 ... The argument is this – from the very beginning of the world God has displayed His divinity to the Gentiles by the testimony of His creation, if not by the preaching of men. Although the Gospel was not heard at that time among the Gentiles, yet the whole workmanship of heaven and earth spoke and proclaimed its Author by its preaching. It is, therefore, clear that, even during the

[3]Ezr. 1:1; Gn. 20:3; 37:5; Dn. 2:1, 29ff.; 2 Ki. 5:17; Dn. 5:5; Nu. 22:9.
[4]Gn. 32:24–30; Jos. 5:13f.; Gn. 16:7–9; 19:1f.; *cf.* Acts 10:30f.
[5]Gn. 12:1 – 25:8; Acts 9:5ff.; Gal. 1:11f.; Acts 16:9ff.; 27:23f.

time in which the Lord confined the favour of His covenant to Israel, He did not withdraw the knowledge of
Himself from the Gentiles, without continually inflaming
some spark of it among them (*Romans*, pp.233f.).

Left to themselves, this cosmic revelation would have en-
gendered in men a knowledge of God's 'eternal power and
divine nature' which, instead of leading them on to worship
and thanksgiving, would have been swallowed up in the
darkness of humanistic philosophy, idolatry and even gross
immorality (Rom. 1:18–32). But did the God who is 'the
Creator and Maker of the whole world' go on 'continually
inflaming some spark [of his grace] among them' *only* that
they might all be 'without excuse', and without any possibility of salvation? May it not be compatible, both with
Scripture and experience, to suggest that God sometimes
so works in men's hearts by his grace that, instead of them
'holding down the truth', he opens their hearts to it and
enables them to embrace such of it as has been revealed to
them?

Is not this, perhaps, the meaning of Peter's words in the
house of Cornelius: 'I now realise how true it is that God
does not show favouritism but accepts men from every
nation who fear him and do what is right' (Acts 10:34f.)?
This cannot mean that the man who tries to be religious
and strives to be moral will earn salvation, for the whole
Bible denies this possibility. But may it not mean that the
man who realizes something of his sin and need, and who
throws himself on the mercy of God with a sincerity which
shows itself in his life (which would always, of course, be a
sure sign of the inward prompting of God's Spirit), would
find that mercy – although without understanding it – at
the cross on which Christ 'died for all' (2 Cor. 5:14)?

'The Apostle', writes G. Campbell Morgan commenting
on this passage, 'did not mean to say that man is received
upon the basis of his morality', for he can be saved only by
what God did in Christ at the cross. 'But no man is to be
saved because he understands the doctrine of the Atonement. He is saved, not by understanding it, but because he
fears God and works righteousness' – and he goes on to
describe 'the glad and glorious surprise' with which, at the

Last Day, we shall find that there are those who have responded to what they knew of divine grace and were 'justified' (acquitted and accepted) 'not because of their morality, but by the infinite merit of the Cross' (*Acts*, p.220).

Romans 3:10–18

In this passage Paul quotes a series of Old Testament verses which provide cumulative evidence that there is no-one on earth who has earned salvation, or could possibly do so, by his own righteousness, understanding, kindness, reverence or search for God. This is basic to the gospel. But it is, perhaps, relevant to observe that the passage is addressed primarily to the Jews (*cf.* v. 19), although verse 9 makes it clear that it is also applicable to the Gentiles. The Bible is explicit in recording the fact that, while all men are sinners and need to be saved by grace, there are some who are *relatively* 'righteous' (*e.g.* Job and Nathanael), and who serve God with what the Old Testament terms 'a perfect heart' – although they fall far short of any objective perfection. So I believe that the statement that 'no one seeks for God' (like the statements that 'their mouths are full of cursing and bitterness' and 'their feet are swift to shed blood') must also be taken in a relative sense:[6] that there is no-one who seeks God perfectly. Is there any convincing reason why the very numerous references and promises in the Scriptures to those who 'seek God' should apply exclusively to those Jews in Old Testament times who responded to God's grace in terms of the Old Covenant, or those who have heard and responded to the gospel? It is true that the asceticism, pilgrimages, prayer and meditation that different religions enjoin, all too often, like Jewish zeal for the Mosaic law, represent man's attempt to earn salvation. But my study of Islam, for example, convinces me that one cannot deny that some of the great Muslim mystics have sought the face of God with a whole-heartedness that cannot be questioned; and I do not doubt that in some cases it was God himself whom they were seeking, not self-justification or a mystical experience *per se*. Like everyone else, they

[6]Like Rom. 1:24–32 and 2 Tim. 3:2–8, this passage depicts human nature in the raw, when not restrained or prompted by either 'common' or 'special' grace.

could be 'saved' by grace alone; but may they not have been responding to some initiative of that grace which was *uniquely* operative in the cross and resurrection of One whose story they had never really heard?

It is at this point that we can, perhaps, see a similarity as well as a difference between those who today have never really heard the gospel and believing Jews under the Old Covenant. What is certain is that no man can earn salvation through his religion, whatever that may be – including, of course, Judaism and Christianity. The difference between the Israelite of old and the 'unevangelized' today is clear: that the former could put his trust in a revelation of God which, though partial and incomplete, was uniquely authoritative. But may there not be a real similarity as well? The believing Jew was accepted and blessed not because of the prescribed animal sacrifices he offered, nor even his repentance and abandonment of himself to God's mercy, but because of what God himself was going to do in his only Son at the cross of Calvary. Of this the Old Testament Israelite had never heard; but this alone could and would provide the moral basis on which God in his forbearance first 'overlooked' his sins (Rom. 3:25) and would finally set him wholly free from them (Heb. 9:15). Somewhat similarly, then, the 'unevangelized' today are (like all mankind) 'prisoners to disobedience' and wholly dependent on whether the 'God of all grace' may so work in their hearts – convicting them of sin and need, awakening a love of the truth, and quickening their faith in whatever he has shown them of his 'purpose of mercy' – that they may be included in the efficacy of the atoning sacrifice, made by a Saviour about whom they have never heard, which was offered, in some sense at least, 'for the sins of the whole world' (1 Jn. 2:2). We can never dogmatize on such a subject, but must rest on the 'depth of wealth, wisdom, and knowledge in God. . . . Source, Guide, and Goal of all that is – to him be glory for ever!' (Rom. 11:33, 36, NEB).

If a man of whom this is true subsequently hears and understands the gospel, then I believe that he would be among the company of those, whom one does sometimes meet on the mission field, who welcome and accept it as soon as they hear it, saying (in effect): 'This is what I have

153

been waiting for all these years. *Why* didn't you come and tell me before?' We must, of course, emphasize the wonderful way in which such people often *have* been brought the message they longed for (*e.g.* Cornelius); but I myself cannot doubt that there may be those who, while never hearing the gospel here on earth, will wake up, as it were, on the other side of the grave to worship the One in whom, without understanding it at the time, they found the mercy of God.

I have recently discussed this point with a well-known writer on comparative religion who emphasizes, just as I do, that salvation can be through Christ alone. He too has struggled with this same problem of whether – and if so how – that salvation can be available to those who, through no fault of their own, have never heard of him; but he takes a more subjective view of the atonement than I do, and insists that the answer must lie in an after-death experience of the transforming power of Christ's love. He observes, reasonably enough, that this cannot properly be termed a 'Second Chance'; for it would represent – at least from one point of view – their first and only chance. But for such a 'chance', whatever one may call it, I can find no warrant in Scripture. Nor do I myself follow his argument; for I dare to believe that if in this world a man has really, as a result of the prompting and enabling of the Holy Spirit, thrown himself on the mercy of God (like the tax-collector in the Temple who cried out 'God be merciful to me, a sinner'), that mercy will already have reached him – on the basis of the propitiation which has been made 'once for all' – and he will have been 'justified'. With much less knowledge he has taken up the same position as the tax-collector who 'did not deserve forgiveness on account of his submissive prayer, but through his self-despising confession of guilt was in a condition to receive the forgiveness granted by God to the penitent. For... the publican the general rule held good that... he who really humbles himself (with sincere confession of guilt) will be exalted' (Geldenhuys, p.451). What will happen to him beyond the grave can best be described, as I see it, as an adoring recognition of his Saviour and a comprehension of what he owes him.

Nor *should* this view, if it be correct, lead to any

diminution of missionary urgency. First, we are under orders, explicit and unequivocal, to go to all the world with the good news. Second, a man such as we have discussed may indeed have found God's mercy, but desperately needs teaching, heart assurance, and a message he can communicate to others. This may, perhaps, be the meaning of the Lord's special message to Paul in Corinth: 'Do not be afraid, but speak...for I have many people in this city' (Acts 18:9f.). On this Campbell Morgan comments that God 'knew the heartache and the agony of many in Corinth... the longing of many, inarticulate, not understood, for exactly that which he [the apostle] had to minister and to give'. The words were not spoken of those who were already Christians, but of 'those whom his Lord numbered among His own' (*Acts*, pp.334f.). Third, if we consider what enabled us ourselves to give up attempting to earn salvation and put our entire trust in the mercy of God, would we not — almost invariably – say that it was hearing the good news of what Christ had done, the very message which the apostle was commanded to preach in Corinth? So it is vitally important that we, too, should go and tell others this same message. Fourth, can we deny others the present experience of joy, peace and power which a conscious knowledge of Christ, and communion with him, alone can bring? As for our own spiritual responsibility *vis-à-vis* the gospel, this is crystal clear, for we *have* heard of the only Saviour, so 'how shall we escape if we neglect such a great salvation?' (Heb. 2:3).

The Jews since the advent of Christ

For some pages now we have been considering the position before God of both believing Israelites under the Old Covenant and those followers of other religions today who have never really heard the gospel. Clearly enough, it behoves Christians to treat all the religions that mean so much to vast numbers of their fellow men with proper respect, and to do their best to understand them. But the question inevitably arises whether Judaism, even today, represents a special case. In one respect at least this is obviously true, for the Christian does not doubt that Israel was the recipient of divine revelations which were both authentic and authoritative, if incomplete and, in some respects, temporary. Nor can he fail to realize that the church will be greatly impoverished if it fails to study the Old Testament. But the question remains: how far does the Jew today represent a special case?

This problem has recently been discussed by the Bishop of Birmingham in a lecture entitled 'The Church and the Jews' (24 February 1983), a printed copy of which he has kindly sent me. Himself a convert from Judaism, Hugh Montefiore is rightly horrified not only by the Nazi Holocaust, as an unparalleled example of cold-blooded genocide, but also by the long centuries of obloquy and persecution which his compatriots have suffered in Christendom in general, and at the hand (or under the influence) of the church in particular. And for this obloquy and persecution, he justly observes, no official body, and no ecumenical Council, has confessed the church's responsibility, shame and penitence.

In evidence of this responsibility he refers both to certain features in the New Testament and a number of positively appalling statements made by Church Fathers – especially Cyprian, Eusebius, Chrysostom and Ambrose. No doubt Judaism was for many years the most implacable opponent of the infant church; but there can be nothing but shame for the venom of these utterly sub-Christian pronouncements. Montefiore is much less convincing, however, when he identifies the genesis of these sentiments in the New Testament, and particularly in Matthew's and John's Gospels and some of Paul's letters.

The denunciations of the 'scribes and Pharisees' in Matthew 23, for example, should never be regarded as all-inclusive in their scope, but as addressed to that predominant group of religious leaders whose obsessive zeal for the minutiae of their legal tradition, and instinctive fear for their own position, made them such inveterate critics of the revolutionary teaching of this upstart reformer — even to the point of plotting his death. That Matthew's record of Jesus' outspoken rebukes betrays 'an atmosphere of hatred' seems to me decisively rebutted by the heartbroken lament over Jerusalem with which this very chapter ends. It seems equally impossible to construe John's references to the fierce opposition Jesus encountered from 'the Jews' as a blanket indictment of the race from which the writer himself almost certainly sprang, into which Jesus was born, and to which he devoted nearly all his ministry. As for Paul, he certainly spoke sharply about the Jewish legalizers who were trying to seduce his converts from the gospel of pure grace, yet he could and did solemnly declare that he could even wish himself to be 'cut off from Christ' for the sake of his fellow Israelites (Rom. 9:3).

There can be no doubt, however, that the Christian church bears the heavy guilt of making it vastly more difficult for a Jew who is proud of his heritage to join the community that has treated his people so shamefully. I well remember a Jewish colleague telling me that Israel was almost unique as a country in which a Jew could embrace Christianity without any suspicion of an ulterior motive. After living for fourteen years in the Middle East, moreover, I know something of the trauma involved in a religious conversion which is regarded as a complete repudiation of one's family, community and culture. This is why Kenneth Cragg has tentatively suggested that in some cases converts from Islam might temporarily forgo individual baptism into the church in order to join a fellowship of 'Lovers of Jesus' in which they could more effectively reach their families and friends (*The Call of the Minaret*, p.349). So we should warmly welcome the fact that today, in parts of America, Jews who accept Jesus as Saviour and Lord think of themselves, and are regarded by their Christian friends, as 'Completed Jews' – thus signifying that, far from repudiating their heritage, they had accepted the Messiah to whom both the Law and the Prophets had pointed.

It is salutary in this context to remember Saul of Tarsus. It was his zeal for what he passionately believed to be the revelation given by God to Moses that prompted him to persecute the infant church, although he must have been deeply impressed by the Christians he hounded, and especially by Stephen's dying prayer for his persecutors. Saul was, indeed, 'kicking against the goads' (Acts 26:14). But he must have said to himself, again and again, 'Jesus *cannot* have been the Messiah, for he was crucified; and the

Law states explictly that "a hanged man is accursed by God'" – that is, that to hang on a gibbet was the fate of one who had come under the 'curse' of breaking God's law) (*cf.* Gal. 3:10, 15). It was only the voice and vision of the risen Lord on the road to Damascus which proved to him beyond doubt that Jesus had been glorified, rather than accursed; and only during his sojourn in Arabia, we may surmise, that the Holy Spirit taught him that the explanation was that Jesus, himself sinless, had been 'made a curse for us'. But if it was only a vision from heaven that brought Saul to whole-hearted surrender, in spite of the Christlike witness of Stephen and others, how much harder it must have been for a convinced Jew during the long centuries when the official church, and countless individuals who professed to be Christians, displayed to Jews only a grotesque mis-representation of the compassionate Saviour they claimed to follow.

Do the Jews, then, represent a special case? James Parkes went so far as to suggest that the Old Covenant remains valid for Jews, while the New Covenant extends the promises of God to Gentiles.[7] But he seems to have ignored the fact that the New Covenant was specifically addressed to 'Israel and Judah' (Je. 31:31). In any case, Montefiore firmly rejects this suggestion, because 'theologically speaking there cannot be one set of truths for Jews and another set of truths for Christians', and because 'the con-cept that the New Covenant is only for Gentiles seems to me to suggest that I, as a Jew, have no place within Chris-tianity – a view to which, perhaps not surprisingly, I take exception'. Equally, he rejects the stance of those who maintain that 'all religions are culturally conditioned and all of them in their different ways point the same way to God', for he cannot accept this 'extreme relativism'. 'All the great religions are to be treated with respect', he says. 'But religions do say different things theologically, and they cannot all be equally true; nor can I accept that there is no such thing as theological truth.'

He also mentions, and courteously rejects, one further theory – that of Rosemary Reuther, who finds the solution to this problem in an outright denial of the eschatological

[7]James Parkes, *Conflict of the Church and Synagogue*.

significance of the historical Jesus. It is, of course, true that the 'present' salvation that Jesus personified and proclaimed is only a foretaste of the eschatological 'Banquet of the Last Days' (*cf.* Rom. 8:8–15; Eph. 1:9f., 13f.; Rom. 11:25f., 32). But to deny that the Messianic Age has even begun in Jesus – so that 'room remains in history for other ways of grace, for many religions, and in particular for the other biblical faith, Judaism' – necessarily involves 'a watered down Christ' which, as Montefiore rightly states, 'a Christian will not tolerate'.

He himself, he says, finds help 'in the doctrine of the Logos, the Word of God, who was incarnate in Jesus Christ, but who also "at sundry times and in divers manners spake in times past unto the fathers by the prophets", and indeed who still speaks today'. This is certainly true; for it was, we are told, 'the Spirit of Christ' who spoke in the Old Testament prophets (1 Pet. 1:11), and whose work it is today to 'convince the world concerning sin and righteousness and judgment' (Jn. 16:8). It may be true, too, that in some sense 'Jesus is the visible embodiment of a divine principle operative in a hidden way in the entire history of men' and that this 'logos theology enables Christians to be open to God's grace operative today in other religions and in secular human history'. But Jesus was infinitely more than the embodiment of a principle, as Montefiore would certainly agree; and we must, I believe, be very careful not to take this 'logos theology' too far. The light of God's truth and the darkness of Satan's deception (and man's consequent fall) are both at work in human history and in 'other religions', as we shall see in the next section of this chapter. In our present context, however, we are not concerned with other religions in general or with Judaism in particular, but with individual Jews whose impressions of Christianity have been grossly distorted by the shameful treatment their nation received from the Christian church during the long centuries since it came to political power under Constantine.

We have already seen that we have no warrant in Scripture to dogmatize about the eternal destiny of individuals in other religions, which must be left to a 'faithful Creator' in the day when 'the secrets of [all hearts] will be laid bare' (1 Pet. 4:19; 1 Cor. 14:25). (*Cf.* p.148, above.) But I have ventured to make certain tentative suggestions about some of those who have never really heard about the salvation that there is in Christ Jesus. So our problem is how this may apply to individual Jews since the coming of Christ. And here, it seems to me, Montefiore's somewhat facile conclusion will not stand, and such Jews could, perhaps, be said to fall into four possible categories.

First, while the vast majority of such Jews must have heard the name of Jesus, a considerable number of them may not have heard it in any meaningful way, or may have heard about him in such a distorted form (partly because of their own traditional teaching, and partly because of the impact of the persecution to which they have been subjected), that their position must be much the same as that of people who have not heard at all. Such Jews can scarcely be said realistically to have *rejected* Christ, and their position may perhaps be somewhat similar to that of those who lived under the Old Covenant. This means that they could never earn salvation 'by observing the law, because by observing the law no-one will be justified' (Gal. 2:16); but any who, by the effective prompting of the Holy Spirit, are enabled to respond in repentance and faith to God's promises of grace in the Old Testament would presumably be saved, like their believing ancestors, not by the pristine symbols of atonement, which were ineffective and had to be repeated year by year, but by the final atonement made once for all by Christ (Heb. 9:15). On this Calvin comments: 'If anyone asks whether the sins of the fathers were remitted under the Law, we must hold . . . that they were remitted, but remitted by the mercy of Christ' (Calvin, *Hebrews, ad loc.*).

Second, there are no doubt some Jews who, in spite of their deep alienation from the Christian church as such, come to see Jesus as their promised Messiah, and accept him in their hearts as Saviour and Lord, but feel they cannot commit themselves to the institutional church. Such people choose a lonely path that inevitably means spiritual deprivation — an experience well known, for example, in many Muslim countries to women whose confession of Christ is severely restricted, but not silenced, by their husbands or fathers.

Third, there are all those (whether Jews, nominal Christians or others) who either ignore the challenge of Christ or who face up to it, understand it, and deliberately reject it — whether sadly, because they consider the cost too great, or defiantly, because they prefer to go their own way. About such it still remains written: 'whoever does not believe stands condemned already because he has not believed in the name of God's one and only Son. This is the verdict: Light has come into the world, but men loved darkness instead of light because their deeds were evil' (Jn. 3:18f.). Tragically, such have chosen their destiny.

Happily, however, there is a fourth alternative. There is today an increasing number of Jews who, far from rejecting Christ (or from becoming absorbed in the non-Jewish secular community), accept Jesus as their Messiah, Saviour and Lord and come, as 'Completed' or 'Messianic' Jews, to join some Christian fellowship, and be accepted by it, as those who have in no sense repudiated their Jewish heritage but have followed it to its divinely predicted fulfilment.

An important point should be added. In Romans 11 Paul summarizes, as a matter of divine revelation (v.25), the broad scope of the history of salvation. First, a number of Jews (the 'remnant' of v.5) would come to faith and salvation – both initially, in the apostolic church, and all down the succeeding centuries – while the nation as a whole was 'hardened' in unbelief (vv.7f. and 25), and salvation was proclaimed to all mankind until 'the full number of the Gentiles has come in' (v.25). When this has happened (v.26, NEB) 'all Israel' – that is, 'Israel as a whole', not necessarily every individual Israelite – 'will be saved'. And the quotation that follows in verse 27 (which may well be composite, based on Is. 59:20; Ps. 14:7; Is. 27:9 and Je. 31:33) seems to suggest that this national salvation will be brought about by the appearance (from the heavenly Zion?) of the Deliverer, or Redeemer, in his Parousia (*cf. Romans*, by Cranfield, Matthew Black and Bruce, respectively, *ad loc.*).

Are only a few people going to be saved?

It would, I think, be relevant at this point to return briefly to the question which Jesus 'refused to answer' (to which reference has been made on p.148, above). This question, which represents the sub-title of this section, was not, in point of fact, precisely the same as the question which Newbigin was tackling in that admirable quotation, or which I have been discussing subsequently. The disciples were asking about the *number* of the redeemed, while we have been concerned with their *identity*. But there is no reason to think that Jesus would have given any substantially different answer if the disciples had phrased their question in somewhat different terms; for when Peter asked him a question about John's future ministry, we read that Jesus, in effect, replied: 'That is no business of yours. Your task is to follow me yourself' (*cf*. Jn. 21:20–22). And the two questions are, to be sure, in some sense inter-related.

We have seen that an essential element in God's purpose in the creation of the world was to bring 'many sons to glory' (Heb. 2:10), and that the book of Revelation pictures these sons as 'a great multitude that no-one could count, from every nation, tribe, people and language', all ascribing their salvation 'to our God, who sits on the throne, and to the Lamb' (Rev. 7:9f.). But, however great their *absolute* number may be, the redeemed are commonly thought of as *relatively* few – snatched, as it were, from a perishing world. But is this in fact the clear and unequivocal teaching of Scripture? There are certainly many passages which give us this impression, but it is by no means certain that these passages represent the full picture.

The primary reason for this widespread impression is probably the distinctly indirect answer that Jesus did give, in Luke 13:24f., to his disciples' question. 'Make every effort to enter the narrow door,' he said, 'because many, I tell you, will try to enter and will not be able to.' And he is recorded in Matthew 7:13f. as giving almost exactly the same exhortation in rather more detail: 'Enter through the narrow gate. For wide is the gate and broad is the road that leads to destruction, and many enter through it. But small is the gate and narrow the road that leads to life, and only a few find it.' It seems clear, therefore, that in declining to answer their question in any direct or theoretical way, his purpose was deliberately to turn their minds from abstract speculation about the ultimate ratio between the number of the redeemed and that of the reprobate to the practical question of their own duty to 'press toward the mark' (as Paul subsequently put it) by choosing a 'gate' that would inevitably mean renunciation and self-denial and a 'road' that would at times prove both arduous and lonely.

This it appears, was certainly the major thrust of his exhortation and warning, the essence of which was to discourage any superficial discipleship or light-hearted drifting with the crowd. But B. B. Warfield has pertinently remarked, in an essay on this very subject,[8] that the parable of the Ten Bridesmaids can scarcely be pressed to the point of suggesting that the number of those who will ultimately be welcomed into the Wedding Feast will be exactly equal to that of those who will be shut out; or that the parable of the Wheat and Weeds must be taken to imply any particular ratio between the wheat itself and the weeds that must first be gathered up out of the 'field' which represents the world before the wheat can be finally garnered.

At the time when Jesus spoke these words the number of his disciples was certainly very small. And there have, indeed, been long periods of time, and vast areas of the world, in which Christian witness, all down the ages, has been exceedingly sparse, and visible results negligible. But there have also been times of revival and blessing; and who can tell how some of God's promises are still going to be fulfilled?

How often have missionaries in Egypt, for example, stayed their souls on the prophetic word 'Blessed be Egypt my people' (Is. 19:25; *cf.* vv. 18–25), or those called to witness to Muslims on the promises about Ishmael (Gn. 17:18–21. *Cf.* Kidner, p. 130)? Who would have believed, even a few years ago, that the number of Christians (and, still more, of new converts) in South America and Africa would today greatly outnumber those in Europe and North America? When one realizes the positively astronomical increase in world population in recent years, and its predicted con-

[8]'Are They Few That Be Saved?'

tinuance, comparative statistics become almost meaningless. And if the 'rejection' of Israel meant 'the reconciliation of the world', then 'what will their acceptance be but life from the dead?' (Rom. 11:15). But this glorious prospect must, of course, be balanced by reference to those prophecies which predict a time of increasing evil and apostasy before the end, and to our Lord's question: 'When the Son of Man comes, will he find faith on the earth?' (Lk. 18:8).

There are also quite a number of passages in the Bible that have a distinctly 'universalist' tinge. These are so heavily outweighed by other statements which cannot possibly, as I understand them, be interpreted in any fully universalist sense that we are apt to ignore them. On the face of it, however, the parable of the Yeast teaches that ultimately this 'worked all through the dough' (Mt. 13:33), and that of the Mustard Seed that it would grow to immense proportions (Mt. 13:31f.). In other words, we find in the Bible what seems at first sight a double line of teaching which must either be resolved in some convincing way or else held together in tension. Further passages which demand consideration in this context include John 3:17–21, which at one and the same time asserts that 'God did not send his Son into the world to condemn the world, but to save the world through him', and yet makes it clear that those who 'prefer' darkness to the light of Christ 'stand condemned already'; and 1 John 2:2 where, after the reference in the previous verse to our Advocate, 'Jesus Christ, the Righteous One', the writer continues: 'He is the atoning sacrifice for our sins' and then adds, 'and not only for ours but also for the sins of the whole world'.

About this verse Howard Marshall comments: 'The universal provision implies that all men have need of it. There is no way to fellowship with God except as our sins are forgiven by virtue of the sacrifice of Jesus. At the same time John rules out the thought that the death of Jesus is of limited efficacy; the possibility of forgiveness is cosmic and universal' (Marshall, p.119). There are, of course, those who make a clear-cut distinction here between Christ's propitiation, which concerns 'the whole world', and his advocacy, which exclusively concerns 'those who believe' –

with the implication that it is only his advocacy which makes the propitiation effective. But this really will not do, for 'The efficacy of the advocacy rests on that of the propitiation, not the efficacy of the propitiation on that of the advocacy. It was in the propitiatory death of Christ that John finds Christ's saving work: the advocacy is only its continuation – its unceasing presentation in heaven... And this saving work is common to Christians and "the whole world".' So, if we 'do not attempt the impossible feat of emptying the conception of "propitiation" of its content, this means that in some sense what is called a "universal atonement" is taught in this passage. The expiatory efficacy of Christ's blood extends to the entire race of mankind' (Warfield, 'Jesus Christ the Propitiation for the Whole World', pp.173f., 171).

But other passages in the Bible (*e.g.* Jn. 3:18f. quoted above) teach explicitly that those who prefer darkness to the light will not benefit from Christ's propitiatory death, and that those who reject his claims will 'die in their sins' (Jn. 8:24) – and verses of substantially identical import could be multiplied. In other words, 1 John 2:2 represents 'universal atonement' only '*in some sense*'. So the question is: in what sense? To this question Abraham Kuyper, the great Dutch theologian, replies that

From this difficulty there is no escape, until special Revelation is no longer viewed as directed soteriologically to individual man. Revelation goes out to *humanity* taken as a whole.... By this we do not deny the soteriological aim of special Revelation, but merely assert that salvation of the individual soul is not its rule. Its standard is and will be theological; its first aim is *theodicy*. Surely whoever believes on Christ shall be saved; this is possible first and only because God sent his Son; but the aim, and therefore also end, of all this is, to make us see how God has loved *His* world, and that therefore the creation of this cosmos, even in the face of sin, has been no *failure*.... The subject of [God's] action is not the individual person, but the general Ego of believing humanity – a limitation in which the additional term of 'believing' is no contradiction, if only it is understood

165

how wrong it is to suppose that the real stem of humanity shall be lost, and merely an aggregate of elect individuals shall be saved. On the contrary, it should be confessed that in hell there is only an aggregate of lost individuals, who were cut off from the stem of humanity, while humanity as an *organic whole* is saved.... By 'believing humanity', therefore, we understand the human race as an organic whole, so far as it *lives,* i.e. so far as unbelief has turned again to faith or shall turn (Kuyper, pp.281–284).

In his Essay on 'Are They Few That Be Saved?' Warfield makes a very passing reference to part of this quotation and then translates from the Dutch a passage in another of Kuyper's books in which he 'finely says':

Ask whether God has deserted since the fall this, His splendid creation, this human race with all its treasure of His image, – in a word, *this His world,* in order that, casting it aside, He may create *an entirely new somewhat* out of and for the elect. And the answer of the Scriptures is a decided negative... If we liken mankind, thus, as it has grown up out of Adam, to a tree, then the elect are not leaves which have been plucked off from the tree that there may be braided from them a wreath for God's glory, while the tree itself is to be felled, rooted up, and cast into the fire; but precisely the contrary, the lost are the branches, twigs, and leaves which have fallen away from the stem of mankind, while the elect alone remain attached to it. Not the stem itself goes to destruction, leaving only a few golden leaflets strewn on the field of eternal light, but, on the contrary, the stem, the tree, the race abides, and what is lost is broken from the stem and loses its organic connection.

As I understand these quotations – and Kuyper's writings, for all his massive intellect, acute perception, 'Reformed' orthodoxy and periodical eloquence, are not easy reading – Kuyper is not concerned with the ratio between the redeemed and the reprobate (indeed, he sees himself bound to explain, Warfield observes, 'that the tree of humanity which abides may be, and in point of fact is, less in actual mass than the branches which are broken off'), but with the basic postulate that it is humanity as an organic entity which is redeemed, and that it is 'all things, whether things on earth or things in heaven', that God did in principle 'reconcile to himself by making peace through [Christ's] blood, shed on the cross' (Col. 1:20).

Curiously enough, Robert J. Breckinridge, an American Reformed theologian of a slightly earlier vintage – writing from what Warfield describes as 'an apparently opposite standpoint (verbally at least)' – disagrees with Kuyper on two points. He asserts that

> The human race is not a restored race, out of which a certain number are lost; but it is a fallen race out of which a certain number are saved. It is logically immaterial what the proportions of the lost and saved to the whole race, and to each other, may be; but the question as to the mode is vital as regards the possibility of any salvation at all . . . The race is lost, with a portion of it – far the greater portion it may be – saved through the free, sovereign, efficacious, special grace of God (Breckinridge, p.513).

But we are not concerned here with numbers; and I doubt if Kuyper and Breckinridge are as flatly opposed to each other as it might appear in regard to the basic question of the mode of salvation. In any case it seems to me that Kuyper's way of putting the matter, in relation both to humanity as a race and the world as a whole, has strong biblical support in the verses I have already quoted. Human beings are certainly fallen creatures; and the 'world' as we know it is still, largely, 'under the control of the evil one' (1 Jn. 5:19). But God has already, in principle, reconciled 'all things, whether things on earth or things in heaven' (significantly with no mention here of 'things under the earth') to himself by the atoning sacrifice and victory of the cross (cf. Col. 1:20; 2:15), where 'Jesus Christ, the Righteous One' (1 Jn. 2:1) took away 'the sin of the world' (cf. Jn. 1:29). Yet it is only when he comes again that the 'sheep' will be separated from the 'goats', and that we shall see 'everything made subject' to the One who 'tasted death for everyone'

(Heb. 2:8f.). In other words, God has declared his gracious amnesty, and now calls on all men to respond, to avail themselves of this amnesty, and to come out of their rebellion into glad allegiance.

It is, of course, only by the prevenient grace of God that even those who hear about this 'amnesty' can respond. But what about infants? Warfield states that most 'Reformed thinking' – and, indeed, 'the thinking of the Christian world' – seems to be 'converging' to the view that 'All that die in infancy will be saved', adding that this could only be 'through the almighty operation of the Holy Spirit who worketh when and where and how he pleaseth' (*Studies in Theology*, p.444) – on the basis, no doubt, of 'the atoning sacrifice' of the Lord Jesus Christ 'for the sins of the whole world' (1 Jn. 2:2). So what of more mature persons who have sinned consciously, but have never heard (and are therefore in no position to accept with explicit faith) the gospel of God's matchless love for the whole world? May it not be that 'God our Saviour, who wants all men to be saved' (1 Tim. 2:4), and does not want 'anyone to perish' (2 Pet. 3:9), quickens in some men by his Spirit a consciousness of sin and need, and enables them, in the twilight, to cast themselves on his mercy? If so, then they, too, would be saved by the grace of God in Christ alone.

Only yesterday I read the story of a missionary who, stopping by the roadside to drink some coffee, was confronted by an illiterate herdsman who asked her: 'Are you a sent one, by the Great God, to tell me of a thing called Jesus?' His brother, it appeared, had heard a visiting speaker, at the school at which he was a teacher, tell the children that he had been sent to them by a great God to tell them about 'something called Jesus'. Not interested himself, he had gone out for a drink; but 'every day since', his illiterate brother said, 'I've repeated the phrase: "A sent one from a great God to tell them about something called Jesus": and each time I said the word "Jesus", it was sweet in my heart. So I began to want to know more' (Roseveare, pp.101f.).

By the providence of God the missionary had stopped, and was able to lead him (like Cornelius) into the knowledge and assurance of salvation. But supposing she had not responded in this way to her need to ward off drowsiness – which was, no doubt, the unrecognized prompting of the Holy Spirit – would that 'seeker' have been eternally lost? And supposing the special speaker had never visited the school, would that herdsman have been a seeker at all?

But 'supposing' things like this is a fool's game. As in Jesus' reply to Peter's question about John, that is not our business. Our duty is to obey and be his witnesses; our commission is to 'go and make disciples of all nations' (Mt. 28:19); and our message is a call to radical repentance and the good news of God's free forgiveness in Christ. We are called to action, not speculation.

Non-Christian religions as such

Turning from individuals to other religions as such, what view should the Christian take of non-Christian religions – other than Old Testament Judaism – as systems which profess to mediate salvation? Many different answers have been given to this question; but, broadly speaking, three main views have been – and still are – held by Christians.

First, there are those who, impressed by the element of truth that can be found in most, if not all, other religions, and by the devotion and virtue of some of their adherents, regard them as a sort of *praeparatio evangelica* – as, indeed, all Christians would say of Old Testament Judaism. Christ, therefore, comes 'not to destroy but to fulfil'; and the convert ought to feel that 'he has lost nothing but has gained much, and that in particular all that was true in his old allegiance has been preserved' – and, indeed, enhanced – 'in the new' (Allen, *Christianity among the Religions*, p.123).

Some who take this view would, as we have seen, explain the elements of truth in other religions in terms of an original revelation which has never been wholly lost or forgotten. Others, again, would discern in them the work of Christ himself, as the eternal Logos and the 'light that enlightens every man'. It is he, they would say, who 'bears witness to, makes manifest, the eternal truth which is written on the heart of man as such' (Allen, p.35). As

169

William Temple put it: 'By the word of God – that is to say by Jesus Christ – Isaiah and Plato, Zoroaster, Buddha, and Confucius uttered and wrote such truths as they declared. There is only one Divine Light, and every man in his own measure is enlightened by it' (Temple, vol. I, p.10).

This view was held by Justin Martyr and the Christian philosophers of Alexandria in the second and third centuries (*cf.* Dewick, p.120) and has been adopted by many others down the years. In E. L. Allen's summary of Schelling's thought, Christ 'was present in every age to every race, but he was not known as such. Heathenism is related to Christianity as law to gospel, reason to faith, nature to grace. The heathen is like a blind man, feeling the sun's warmth but not seeing the sun itself. Christ was within heathenism as natural potency but not yet as a personal principle' (Allen, p.70). It was only when the Word was made flesh, however, that he could be known as a personal Saviour and Lord.

This approach to the subject was widely held in Protestant missionary circles in the early years of this century and is amply documented in the volume of the Edinburgh Conference of 1910 on *The Missionary Message*. Thus other religions can be seen as a preparation for the gospel either as the 'revelation of deep wants of the human spirit' which the gospel alone can fully satisfy, or as 'partial insights which are corrected and completed by the gospel'. The main objection to this view is that, in R. Otto's phrase, 'the different religions turn on different axes. They simply do not ask or answer the same questions' (*cf.* Newbigin, *The Open Secret*, pp.193f.).

A variant but related approach to the same matter, dominant at the Jerusalem Conference of 1928, was to seek and acknowledge specific 'values' in the different religions, and to claim that it is in Christianity alone that all these values 'are found in their proper balance and relationship'. And yet, as the statement itself says: 'Christ is not merely the continuation of human traditions: coming to him involves the surrender of the most precious traditions. The "values" of the religions do not together add up to him who alone is the truth' (Newbigin, *op. cit.*, p.194).

The second view which has been taken by Christians

about other religions is the diametrical opposite of this: namely, that they do not emanate in any sense from God, but from the devil. Prominence is given, therefore, to the darker side of their ethical teaching and the least acceptable elements in their theological concepts; and those rays of truth which they indubitably contain are explained in terms of the fact that even Satan himself can and does sometimes appear as an angel of light (2 Cor. 11:14). A primary emphasis is put on the basic fact that they inevitably deny – whether by explicit statement, as in Islam, or by implicit teaching, as in the great pre-Christian religions – the unique claims of the 'Word made flesh', and that they hold themselves out, as it were, as substitutes for and alternatives to the only gospel that can save and satisfy. And if this view strikes many of us as much too extreme, it is well to take heed to two observations made in this context by Lesslie Newbigin. First, he remarks that there is at least an element of truth here: 'the sphere of religions is the battlefield *par excellence* of the demonic. New converts often surprise missionaries by the horror and fear with which they reject the forms of their old religion – forms which to the secularized Westerner are interesting pieces of folklore and which to the third-generation successors of the first converts may come to be prized as part of national culture.'

Secondly, he insists that this 'strange idea' points to another important truth. For 'it is precisely at points of highest ethical and spiritual achievement that the religions find themselves threatened by, and therefore ranged against, the gospel. It was the guardians of God's revelation who crucified the Son of God. It is the noblest among the Hindus who most emphatically reject the gospel. It is those who say, "We see", who seek to blot out the light (John 9:41)' (Newbigin, *op. cit.*, pp.192f.).

The third view sees these religions as not so much divine revelation, nor yet Satanic deception, but as human aspiration – as man's attempts (whether more or less enlightened) to solve the mysteries of life. Among those who take this view there are two possible attitudes with regard to Christianity itself. Some would regard it as no more than the nearest approximation to ultimate truth, man's highest attainment in the age-long evolution of religion. Others

171

would go much further than this, and believe it to be the one and only divine self-disclosure (with Judaism, of course, as a forerunner), in which God himself came down from heaven, as it were, to reveal himself to man, while all the other religions represent human attempts to climb up to heaven to discover God.

I cannot, myself, opt for any one of these three views *simpliciter*, for there is, I believe, some truth in each. The non-Christian religions seem to me to resemble a patchwork quilt, with brighter and darker components in differing proportions. There are elements of truth which must come from God himself, whether through the memory of an original revelation, through some process of cross-fertiliz-ation with some other religion, or through that measure of self-disclosure which, I cannot doubt, God still vouchsafes to those who truly seek him (*cf*. pp.145–155, above). But there are also elements which are definitely false, and which I, for one, believe come from 'the father of lies' – whose primary purpose is not so much to entice men into sensual sin as to keep them back, by any means in his power, from the only Saviour. Yet again, there is much that could best be described as human aspirations after the truth, rather than either divine revelation or Satanic deception.

But is there, as some would assert, any 'saving structure' in these other religions? To this question the papal encyclical *Ecclesiam Suam* (1964) seems to give no sort of answer, for it simply envisages humanity as ranged in concentric circles with the Roman Catholic Church at the centre and with other Christians, Jews, Muslims, other theists, other religionists, and then atheists at progressively greater distances. But recent Roman Catholic writings, such as those of Karl Rahner and Hans Küng, go much farther than this (*cf*. pp.24f., 32f., above), with their doctrines of 'relative validity' and 'anonymous Christians'. To put the point more sharply, can we say, with Raymond Panikkar, that the 'good and bona fide Hindu is saved by Christ and not by Hinduism, but it is through the sacraments of Hinduism, through the message of morality and the good life, through the mysterion that comes down to him through Hinduism, that Christ saves the Hindu normally' (Pan-nikar, p.54. *Cf*. pp.35, 147f., above)? For myself, I could not go nearly so far as this[9], and think there is much more truth in a dictum of W. Cantwell Smith that 'If there is any truth in the Buddhist tradition, then its truth is not "in Buddhism", it is in the nature of things' (*The Faith of Other Men*, p.81) – for we are all one in our basic human need. I have heard of more than one Muslim whose study of the Qur'ān made him seek after Christ[1]; but I think we must ascribe this to the Spirit of God meeting him in his need, rather than attribute it to the Qur'ān as such. Yet there are certainly elements in non-Christian religions – and, indeed, in the heart of man – that testify in some measure to the righteousness and judgment of God, to the sin and guilt of man, and to the need of men and women everywhere for expiation and forgiveness, through all of which God can speak.

In other words, God has never left himself wholly without witness in his self-disclosures to mankind (James, *Christianity*, p.154. *Cf.* Acts 14:17). This is true even of those who stifle or 'suppress' the truth, as Paul insists (Rom. 1:18). It is true of the Muslim, who believes passionately in one true God, however much we may regard his concept of that God as in many ways a caricature of the 'God and Father of our Lord Jesus Christ' – for I have never met a Muslim convert who regards the God he previously sought to worship as a wholly false God. Instead, he is filled with wonder and gratitude that he has now been brought to know that God as he really is, in Jesus Christ our Lord. And this is still more evident, as we have seen, in converts from Judaism who, like Paul before Felix, testify (in one phrase or another) that according to the 'Way', which other Jews called a sect, they now worship the God of their fathers (Acts 24:14), uniquely and finally revealed in Christ. 'This element of continuity', as Lesslie Newbigin writes, 'is confirmed in the experience of many who have become converts to Christianity from other religions. Even though this conversion involves a radical discontinuity, yet there is often the strong conviction afterwards that it was the living and true God who was dealing with them in

---

[9] *Cf.*, in particular, Newbigin's words quoted on pp. 147f., above.
[1] *E.g.* a certain Mallam Ibrāhīm, who was crucified in the market place in Kano nearly a century ago.

the days of their pre-Christian wrestlings' (*The Finality of Christ*, p.59).

But now, in Christ, the one eternal God has actually become man. He has not merely visited humanity, he has taken our very nature. Now there is only one teacher, one Lord, one shepherd, one mediator (*cf.* Hooft, p.96). He has a name which is above every name. 'In no one else can salvation be found. For in all the world no other name has been given to men but this, and it is by this name that we must be saved!' (Acts 4:12, Phillips). So the attitude of the Christian to men of other religions can only be the attitude of the 'witness who points to the one Lord Jesus Christ as the Lord of all men ... The Church does not apologise for the fact that it wants all men to know Jesus Christ and to follow him. Its very calling is to proclaim the Gospel to the ends of the earth. It cannot make any restrictions in this respect. Whether people have a high, a low or a primitive religion, whether they have sublime ideals or a defective morality makes no fundamental difference in this respect. All must hear the Gospel' (Hooft, p.116).

And this is a call for radical repentance and conversion. 'When the people heard the first Christian preaching they were cut to the heart and said to Peter: "What shall we do?" Peter said, "Repent, be baptized every one of you in the name of Jesus Christ for the forgiveness of your sins and you shall receive the Holy Spirit. The promise is to you and your children and to all that are afar off, every one whom the Lord calls." That does not mean, however, that the promise does not need to be accepted. There is an RSVP on this card. "And those who received the word were baptized ... and they devoted themselves to the apostles' teaching and fellowship, to the breaking of the bread and the prayers"' (Newbigin, *The Finality of Christ*, p.99).

Addendum

Since writing the manuscript of this book, I have read (just today) a sincere and sensitive book (entitled *God, That's Not Fair!*) by Dick Dowsett, of the Overseas Missionary Fellowship, in which he takes a distinctly different view from mine in regard to part of this chapter. Again and again, however, I find myself in deep agreement with him. We are, indeed, involved in a world in which millions are living and dying without any knowledge of the salvation that there is in Christ alone. In this life most people think they can get by without him; but one day all will come to the awful realization that they were wrong. The issue is as stark as it could be: eternal life or eternal death – and it is our duty to make this known, and to point people to him. I very much wish I had myself done this more effectively, and been more faithful in prayer.

It is true that I should not always express myself in precisely Dick Dowsett's terms, but there is only one major point on which I feel bound to differ from him: namely, that I cannot believe that *all* those who have never heard the gospel are *inevitably* lost. What about all those who have died, and still die, in infancy (*cf.* p.168, above)? As for the more mature, I have no doubt whatever that the presentation of the gospel, by voice or writing, is the normal way by which people are reached and won; but I do not believe that we have any biblical warrant to assert that this is the *only* way. On the contrary, I believe there is much, in the Bible and experience, to point to the fact that God *can*, and sometimes does, work directly in men's hearts to convict them of sin and prompt them to throw themselves on his mercy.

Needless to say, my views (although shared, I know, by many others) are my responsibility alone. And I very much hope that many people will read Dick Dowsett's book – to confirm the many points on which we agree, to ponder the few points on which we differ, and (above all) to take to heart his resounding challenge.

6

Proclamation, dialogue, or both?

Proclamation

Chapter 2 of this book was devoted to the 'unique proclamation' of the apostolic church and the ways in which it differs from that of other faiths. We saw that the apostles concentrated on recounting, again and again, a historical event which was intimately known to them, and to which they could give their unqualified, personal testimony: the life, words and deeds, and above all the death and resurrection, of One with whom they had kept close company for some three years. The original Twelve were no philosophers and had had no theological training; but they could not be silenced from 'speaking about what we have seen and heard' (Acts 4:20).

At the beginning, this proclamation was confined to the Jews, but in a very short time it was extended to the Samaritans (Acts 8:1, 5–25), to individual Gentiles like Cornelius (Acts 10:1 – 11:18), and then, in the Gentile mission which was centred on Antioch, to Cyprus, Asia Minor, Greece, Rome and beyond. On Mars Hill in Athens Paul (a 'Hebrew of Hebrews', who was a Roman citizen by birth, was fluent in Greek and had received the training of a strict Pharisee in Jerusalem) declared that

'The God who created the world and everything in it, and who is Lord of heaven and earth, does not live in shrines made by men...As some of your own poets have said, "We are also his offspring." As God's off-spring, then, we ought not to suppose that the deity is like an image in gold or silver or stone, shaped by human craftsmanship and design. As for the times of ignorance, God has overlooked them; but now he commands man-kind, all men everywhere, to repent, because he has fixed the day on which he will have the world judged, and justly judged, by a man of his choosing; of this he has given assurance to all by raising him from the dead' (Acts 17:24–31, NEB).

Nor did he by any means confine his proclamation to such a formal occasion. On the contrary, 'he reasoned in the synagogue with the Jews and the God-fearing Greeks, as well as in the market-place day by day with those who happened to be there...preaching the good news about Jesus and the resurrection'. It was, indeed, as a result of this street preaching that 'a group of Epicurean and Stoic philosophers...brought him to a meeting of the Areopagus, where they said to him, "May we know what this new teaching is that you are presenting? You are bringing some strange ideas to our ears, and we want to know what they mean"' (Acts 17:16–20).

This visit to Athens gives a clear impression of Paul's basic message, for the effect of his preaching at Thessalonica, a little earlier, had been that a number of people had 'turned to God from idols to serve the living and true God, and to wait for his Son from heaven, whom he raised from the dead – Jesus, who rescues us from the coming wrath' (1 Thes. 1:9f.). In his letter to the Romans, moreover, he explains this reference to 'wrath' in the words:

God has shown us how much he loves us – it was while we were still sinners that Christ died for us! By his death we are now put right with God; how much more, then, will we be saved by him from God's anger! We were God's enemies, but he made us his friends through the death of his Son (Rom. 5:8ff., GNB).

And the fact that both Paul in this passage and John in 1 John 4:10 regarded Christ's atoning death as the supreme demonstration of God's *own* love for us clearly points to an ontological unity between the Father who sent and the Son who came. This essential unity is again emphasized in the summary of apostolic teaching Paul gives in the words: 'there is for us only one God, the Father, who is the Creator of all things and for whom we live; and there is only one Lord, Jesus Christ, through whom all things were created and through whom we live' (1 Cor. 8:6, GNB) – for here the Christians' God and Lord are held intimately together in both person and function.

To the apostolic church it was beyond doubt the resurrection and exaltation of Jesus which provided the conclusive evidence that he was 'both Lord and Christ' (Acts 2:36). In his sermon on the day of Pentecost which ended with these words, Peter had begun by referring to the life and divinely empowered ministry of Jesus as a matter of common knowledge (v. 22), then to his crucifixion by the Romans at the instigation of 'you and your rulers' (v. 23. *Cf*. 3:17) – although he emphasized that even in this terrible act they were unconsciously fulfilling the 'set purpose and foreknowledge' of God (v. 23. *Cf*. 3:18), for it had always been foretold that the Messiah would suffer (*cf*. Lk. 24:25, 46; Acts 17:3; 26:23). But God had 'raised him from the dead . . . because it was impossible for death to keep its hold on him' (v. 24). Of this fact Psalm 16:8–11 is quoted in confirmation as an Old Testament 'testimony', for the Psalmist's words were certainly not applicable to David himself (whose grave was there for all to see, and whose flesh had clearly 'suffered decay'), but they had been fulfilled in 'great David's greater Son', whose soul had not been left in Hades, but exalted to the joy of God's presence. And of the fact that 'this Jesus' had been raised from the dead and exalted by God the apostolic band could all bear their personal testimony (vv. 25–32).

But Peter's hearers had not themselves seen either the risen Christ or his ascension. For these they were dependent on the apostles' witness and the Old Testament testimonies that Peter had just quoted and was about to quote; but they *had* themselves seen some of the external symbols and evidences of the Holy Spirit's presence. So Peter could go on to say that Jesus, exalted by God, 'has received from the

Father the promised Holy Spirit and has poured out what you now see and hear' (v. 33). An Old Testament reference to this new experience of the Spirit's power had already been provided (in vv. 6–21) by a quotation from Joel 2:28–32; and for the fact that Jesus had now been exalted to the right hand of God, the very throne of the universe, there to await his final triumph, Psalm 110:1 is now called in aid (vv. 34f.) – the same verse that had been used by Jesus himself to show that the title 'Son of David is, by itself, an inadequate and misleading description of the Messiah, and that the Old Testament contains intimations that the Coming One will be a far more exalted figure who, instead of merely occupying the throne of David, will share the throne of God' (Caird, *The Gospel of Luke*, p.226). So Peter aptly concludes his sermon with the words: 'Let all Israel then accept as certain that God has made this Jesus, whom you crucified, both Lord and Messiah' (v.36, NEB).

Romans 1:3 and 4 provide further evidence for the fact that the early church always regarded the resurrection as the event which proved decisively that Jesus, son of David by human birth, had thereby been openly declared to be both 'Messiah' and 'Son of God with power'. The last two words may either refer to God's 'mighty act' (NEB) in raising Jesus from the dead, or to the fact that he 'who was the Son of God in weakness and lowliness' during his earthly ministry became by the resurrection 'the Son of God in power' (Bruce, *Romans*, p.72, quoting A. Nygren, *ad loc.*). So the apostle adds the words: 'Jesus Christ our Lord' (v. 4), which echo what was almost certainly the church's earliest credal formula, 'Jesus is Lord' (Rom. 10:9; 1 Cor. 12:3. *Cf.* Phil. 2:11; 1 Pet. 3:15). And in Acts 13:33 Paul is recorded as quoting Psalm 2:7 ('You are my Son; this day have I begotten you') as fulfilled in the resurrection – not because Jesus *became* God's Son by being raised from the dead, but rather that it was to prove that he was his Son that God raised him.

No doubt the confession of Jesus as 'Lord' by Paul and others 'was *informed* [my italics] by their acquaintance with other contenders for that title'. It is certainly true, as Frances Young writes, that they contrasted their Lord with Lord Caesar and with the Lords of contemporary mystery-cults. They could not have communion with their Lord's table and also that of some other Lord (1 Cor. 10:21). Unlike their neighbours who confessed gods many and lords many, they affirmed one God and one Lord (1 Cor. 8:5–6). The Lord Christ was exalted at God's right hand; he had been given the name that is above every other name, Kyrios (Phil. 2:11).[1]

But surely the most noteworthy fact about this last verse is that Paul himself, or a still earlier tradition which he quotes, 'boldly transfers to Jesus a great monotheistic passage from Isa. 45:23, in which God is represented as declaring that he must have no rivals: it is now to *Kurios Iesous Christos* that every knee shall bow, and it is he whom every tongue shall confess' (Moule, *The Origin of Christology*, pp.41f.).

In point of fact this is only one example of a phenomenon we have already noted: Old Testament quotations, all of which in origin clearly referred to Yahweh, being applied by Christians, from a very early date, to Christ. No doubt this transfer was facilitated by the fact that both the 'tetragrammaton' (or the sacred, covenant name of God) and also the term *'adōnāy* (with special pointing), which was regularly substituted for it when the Scriptures were quoted or read aloud in Hebrew, were translated *'Kyrios'* in the Septuagint – and it seems to me almost perverse to look anywhere other than the Greek Scriptures for the source or implications of this title, when used by Paul or the writers of other New Testament Epistles. It is true that the same Greek word is also used of a human master, owner or overlord, but its divine *overtones* (especially when used in the absolute) were such that 'Jewish rebels, so Josephus tells us, refused to call the Caesar "lord", because they "held God alone to be the Lord"' (Deissmann, p.355); and we know how costly Christians found it to resist this same imposition. Both Christians and Jews, moreover, were fiercely opposed to the syncretism of Greek or Roman mythology and also to that of the contemporary mystery cults.

[1]Frances Young, in *The Myth of God Incarnate*, p.20.

But even in some of these instances of 'the transfer to Christ of passages originally relating to God', Moule observes, 'special care seems to be taken to safeguard, as it were, the supremacy of God. Thus, in Phil. 2:11, the acclamation of Christ in terms originally intended for God is said to be "to the glory of God the Father". Similarly, in Rev. 5:9f., 12f., explicit references to God are brought in alongside of expressions of the worthiness of the Lamb' (Moule, *op. cit.*, pp.42f.). This seems to me wholly consonant with the tenor of 1 Corinthians 8:6, to which reference has already been made, and also to the prologue to John's Gospel: 'In the beginning was the Word, and the Word was with God, and the Word was God. He was with God in the beginning. Through him all things were made; without him nothing was made that has been made. In him was life, and that life was the light of men' (Jn. 1:1–4).

In this context I am forcefully reminded of the debate, at a considerably later date, between the Mu'tazila and the more 'orthodox' Muslims about whether the Qur'ān, as God's word, was really 'eternal' and 'uncreated', as the orthodox have always held. To take this view, the Mu'tazila insisted, was to cease to be a monotheist, since the 'uncreated' and 'eternal' must necessarily be divine. And to this argument the orthodox could, finally, only reply that the Qur'ān, as the Word of God, was '*lā dhātahu wa lā ghayrahu*' – 'neither *identical* with the divine Essence, *nor other than it*' (my italics). To remind a Muslim of this always provides an apt introduction to John 1:1–3.

From the very beginning of the Christian era, therefore, there was the most clamant call for the Christian message to be proclaimed far and wide – to Jews and Samaritans, Greeks and 'barbarians'. Some knew a little, but had traditional reserves and newly acquired misconceptions; some were wistful and even prepared for the message; others were bitterly opposed. But in any and every case hear it they must. It was for this reason that Paul wrote:

To the Jews I became like a Jew, to win the Jews. To those under the law I became like one under the law (though I myself am not under the law), so as to win those under the law. To those not having the law I became like one

181

not having the law (though I am not free from God's law but am under Christ's law), so as to win those not having the law. To the weak I became weak, to win the weak. I have become all things to all men so that by all possible means I might save some. I do all this for the sake of the gospel (1 Cor. 9:20–23).

Nor did he shrink from persecution, hardships and suffering in this vital task of proclamation, for he once felt compelled to tell a story that he was obviously reluctant to spell out.

Five times I received from the Jews the forty lashes minus one. Three times I was beaten with rods, once I was stoned, three times I was shipwrecked, I spent a night and day in the open sea, I have been constantly on the move. I have been in danger from rivers, in danger from bandits, in danger from my own countrymen, in danger from Gentiles; in danger in the city, in danger in the country, in danger at sea; and in danger from false brothers. I have laboured and toiled and have often gone without sleep; I have known hunger and thirst and have often gone without food; I have been cold and naked . . . (2 Cor. 11:24–27).

No-one, surely, could have been more eager, or more absolutely determined, to proclaim the message of Christ to all who would listen to it. When he had the opportunity, he no doubt preached at length – on one occasion until midnight (when one of his audience, 'completely overcome by sleep, fell from the third floor'!); for preaching, as Calvin justly remarked, 'is the normal mode which the Lord has appointed for imparting his Word'. But he also committed the same message to writing by dictating it to an amanuensis in a whole series of letters which have proved of inestimable value to the church.

Basically, moreover, his message was simple. Although it seems to me absurd to suggest that Paul was 'not interested' in the life and teaching of Jesus of Nazareth – a suggestion which is in fact belied by a whole series of almost incidental references – there can be no doubt that his primary emphasis was on 'Christ crucified', for he could write to the Galatians that Jesus Christ had been 'posted up, placarded' as crucified before their very eyes by his preaching (Gal. 3:1, J. B. Lightfoot, p.134). But he continually insisted that the crucified Saviour was now the living Lord, who could and would save his people from their sins; and that God's Spirit was at work in them, progressively to conform them to Christ's own likeness. Already all who responded to God's effectual call had been 'justified' (that is, would be 'acquitted' on the coming Day of Judgment, and were enjoying that status even now[2]), were in the process of being 'sanctified', and could be sure of their future glorification when their Lord came back in salvation and in judgment.

Argumentation

But Paul could listen as well as preach. We have already seen that in Athens he 'argued in the synagogue with the Jews and gentile worshippers, and also in the city square every day with casual passers-by' (Acts 17:17, NEB). A little earlier we read that at Beroea 'The Jews here were more liberal-minded than those at Thessalonica: they received the message with great eagerness, studying the scriptures every day to see whether it was as they said' (Acts 17:11). And this sort of thing went on all his life, for we read that when he had been brought to Rome as a prisoner, but was allowed to lodge by himself under military guard, he called the local Jewish leaders together, and they 'arranged to meet Paul on a certain day, and came in even larger numbers to the place where he was staying. From morning till evening he explained and declared to them the kingdom of God and tried to convince them about Jesus from the Law of Moses and from the Prophets. Some were convinced by what he said, but others would not believe' (Acts 28:16f., 23f.)

Nor is it only among those with whom one can reason from the Scriptures that explanation, and the give and take of argument, play an essential part both in evangelism and in the pastoral ministry. In one sense, the less someone

[2]*Cf.* C. K. Barrett, *Romans*, pp.24ff., 170f.

knows the more questions he may need to ask, and the more explanation may be necessary. I wrote the phrase 'the give and take of argument' advisedly, since the benefit should always – ideally, at least – be mutual. The Christian has the opportunity to help his friend by explaining what he has previously proclaimed; by doing his best to dispel any misunderstandings or misconceptions; and by giving greater substance to those matters of history, doctrine or experience to which he has referred. But he himself also gains greatly from his friend's clarification of his own convictions – how he has come to them and what they mean to him – in a way that enables the Christian to appreciate these convictions with a new sympathy and understanding. He will, too, inevitably be challenged to ask himself some searching questions about what *his* faith really means to him, and whether both his own comprehension and his verbal communication of some of its contents may not be faulty or inadequate. This sort of argument is, indeed, the very situation from which what is commonly termed 'Dialogue' today usually finds its genesis.

Dialogue

It is a profound mistake, therefore, to imagine – and, still more, to postulate – that those who want to participate in a fruitful dialogue must endeavour to come to it with blank minds, or to suppress their personal convictions or distinctive testimony. As Visser 't Hooft aptly put it:

> Martin Buber, who has given us what is probably the most profound analysis of the nature of dialogue, has made it very clear that the presupposition of genuine dialogue is not that the partners agree beforehand to relativise their own convictions, but that they accept each other as persons. In order to enter into a deep relationship with a person the essential requirement is not that he agrees with me, that I agree with him, or that we are both willing to negotiate a compromise, but rather that I turn to him with the willingness to listen to him, to understand him, to seek mutual enrichment. I do not impose my personality on him but put myself at his

disposal with all that I am. As a Christian I cannot do this without reporting to him what I have come to know about Jesus Christ. I shall make it clear that I consider my faith not as an achievement, but as a gift of grace, a gift which excludes all pride, but which obliges me to speak gratefully of this Lord to all who will hear it. I shall be glad also to listen to my partner and may learn much from his account of his spiritual journey.

The dialogue will be all the richer, if both of us give ourselves as we are. For the Christian that giving must include witness. It is possible for convinced Christians to enter into true dialogue with convinced Hindus or Muslims or Jews, yes and even syncretists, without giving up their basic convictions. It should be done in the attitude which Hocking has so well defined as 'reverence for reverence'. The fact that Christians believe that they know the source of divine truth does not mean that they have nothing to learn from men of other faiths. Those of us who have had the privilege of participating in such conversations have often found ourselves humbled and challenged by the evidence we have seen of true devotion, of unflinching loyalty to the truth as they see it among the adherents of other religions (Hooft, pp.117f.)

John Hick, by contrast, insists in his Younghusband Lecture on 'Christian Theology and Inter-Religious Dialogue' (*World Faiths*, pp.2–19) that 'Christianity must move emphatically from the confessional to the truth-seeking stance in dialogue'. But this seemingly liberating suggestion necessarily implies that the individual who engages in dialogue from the stance of profound convictions which he has formulated and tested over years of thought and experience is less concerned for the truth than one who puts his sole emphasis on seeking 'Ultimate Reality', or some equally nebulous phrase. As Newbigin comments:

The latter stance is indicated in the affirmation that 'Transcendent Being is infinitely greater than (one's) own limited view of it'. The former stance might be indicated by such an affirmation as 'Jesus Christ is Lord of all'. Each of these is an affirmation of faith. Neither is an assertion of omniscience. The Christian will also say, 'Jesus Christ is infinitely greater than my limited view of him.' In these respects the two affirmations are analogous. Both are – or can be – made by people who are seriously seeking the truth. The difference lies in the way in which truth is to be sought, the clues which are to be followed, the models by which it is to be grasped, and the weight which is to be given to different kinds of evidence (*The Open Secret*, p.186).

In other words, the individual who adopts what Hick terms the 'confessional' stance starts out – as every thinking man in reality must – from what knowledge he already has, from what his past experience has led him to accept, from what he has thought through for himself and has lived out in company with others, but the basic validity and implications of which he is now prepared to examine – and, if necessary, to adjust – in the light of a truth-seeking dialogue with others whose experiences, meditation and community life have led them to very different conclusions. On any showing this would seem a much more realistic, intelligent and potentially fruitful approach than for both parties to attempt to put all this on one side in favour of some amorphous quest, resting on exceedingly inadequate foundations, of what amounts to little more than a philosophical construction.

In point of fact it is impossible to approach any vital question with a completely open mind – and the more one recognizes and confesses this the more likely one is to avoid misunderstandings. We all, inevitably and instinctively, start from some 'frame of reference'. As Polanyi puts it, 'No intelligence, however critical or original, can operate outside such a fiduciary framework' (*Personal Knowledge*, p.267). In the case of the Christian who enters into dialogue with a non-Christian, this 'fiduciary framework' will be 'an ultimate faith commitment which is honest enough to recognise that it is one among the possible commitments'; and the conversation that results will represent 'a process in which this belief is being constantly reconsidered in the light of the experience of acting it out in every sector of human affairs and in dialogue with every other pattern of thought by which men and women seek to make sense of their lives' (Newbigin, *The Open Secret*, pp.190 and 31).

What, then, is the basic difference between dialogue and argument? To me the difference can be summarized in an illustration which has come home to me in terms of my own experience. In my younger days – whether as a missionary in Egypt, in the course of many tours and contacts in the Muslim world, or in a seminar classroom in London – I often found myself drawn into an argument with Muslim friends or pupils about the relative excellencies of Jesus (*'Īsā*) or Muhammad – or, at a somewhat more sophisticated and perceptive level, about the rival merits of Jesus (as, to the Christian, the supreme revelation of God) and those of the Qur'ān (as representing the summit of revelation to the Muslim). But the trouble with any such argument – necessary though it may sometimes be – is that it is all too easy for both parties to become heated and say things that irritate or even hurt the other. And anything like that, or any spirit of rivalry or competition, inevitably militates against spiritual understanding.

So today I should almost always try to avoid the controversies of the past and make a much more eirenical proposal. 'Don't you think it might be more helpful for us to put argument on this subject on one side', I would say, 'at least for the present? May I ask you instead to tell me, as fully and frankly as you can, what your knowledge of God, as this is ministered to you through the Qur'ān, really means to you? I can promise you that I will listen to what you say with both interest and respect, and that I will make a genuine attempt to understand the nature of that knowledge and its practical implications – trying to stand, as it were, in your shoes. And then, perhaps, you will permit me to tell you, to the best of my ability, what God has come to mean to me as he is revealed in Jesus Christ my Lord.'

This substitution of dialogue for argument has in general, it seems to me, almost everything to commend it. It will help me, as a Christian, to understand a Muslim friend's personal religion – or even the religion of Islam as a whole – much more adequately than any dialectical argument could do. It should not cause any hostility or irritation, for we should both have been exclusively concerned with the effect on our own lives – devotional, moral, social and experimental – of what each of us believes to be God's supreme revelation of himself. In addition, it would almost certainly convict me, on my part, of how little I had really apprehended of 'the gloryof God in the face of Jesus Christ' and how poorly I can communicate even this little to another. And it may, perhaps, have a corresponding effect on my Muslim friend.

In other words, our contact may leave us both changed – and for the better, not the worse. This *can* be, and often is, the result of almost any genuine encounter with some other person. Newbigin has given an admirable New Testament example of this in the whole encounter between Peter and his friends, on the one side, and the relatives and friends of Cornelius, on the other. Neither Peter nor Cornelius was ever the same man again. In the case of Cornelius and those who were with him it led to their radical conversion from being sincere 'seekers' (and even 'God-fearers') to becoming fully convinced Christians, 'speaking in tongues of ecstasy and acclaiming the greatness of God' (Acts 10:44ff., NEB). But Peter, too, had undergone a radical change. The man who two or three days before had said 'No, Lord, no: I have never eaten anything profane or unclean' (Acts 10:14), and who had believed that 'a Jew is forbidden by his religion to visit or associate with a man of another race' (v. 28), was soon to tell the Council of Jerusalem that 'God, who can read men's minds, showed his approval of them by giving the Holy Spirit to them, as he did to us . . . Then why do you now provoke God by laying on the shoulders of these converts a yoke which neither we nor our fathers were able to bear? No, we believe that it is by the grace of the Lord Jesus that we are saved, and so are they' (Acts 15:8–11, NEB).

There are, however, many people today who insist that the very nature and spirit of dialogue are completely destroyed if either of the parties has 'any covert thought for the conversion of the other'. Dialogue, they assert, is simply and solely a matter of sharing — a means of getting to know one another better, of gaining a greater understanding of the faith by which each lives and of exploring some of the pressing (and even agonizing) problems that face us all, in the contemporary world, in the light of what each of these faiths may be able to contribute to their solution. As so often, there is both truth and error, as I see it, in this assertion. It is perfectly true that the primary aim of dialogue is not evangelistic, in the ordinary sense of that term, but that it serves a number of other worthy and useful purposes. It is also true that a large proportion of dialogue could best be regarded as a preparation – a clearing of the ground – for evangelism, rather than its consummation. And it is even more pertinent to remark that a reference to some 'covert' purpose for any Christian activity has a distinctly dubious ring.

Do missionary societies provide equipment and personnel to heal the sick, to prevent the spread of dread diseases, to dig wells, distribute food, and erect shelters for those afflicted by drought, famine or earthquakes, only to exploit physical needs for spiritual purposes? Did the Good Samaritan, as has been aptly asked, take the opportunity to fill the stricken man's pockets with tracts instead of (or even alongside) pouring oil and wine on his wounds, taking him to an inn, and providing money for his care? Missionaries may, no doubt, sometimes have been so intent on their paramount duty and privilege of spreading the good news of eternal salvation that they have viewed everything else, however important, as a means to that supreme end – although not so often when actually face to face with clamant human need, I suggest, than when reviewing their work, or giving an account of it, in retrospect.

In any case, this could scarcely be said of the Good Samaritan, or of the way in which our incarnate Lord himself, 'moved with compassion', met human need at every level – and bade his disciples to do so too. Yet can we doubt that his unswerving purpose was always to do his Father's will – as the Gospel of John continually reiterates? And can we hesitate to believe that in the heart of the Father himself, without whose knowledge not a sparrow falls to the ground, the joy he feels when a lost sheep is found, or a prodigal son finds his way home, is paramount? So how can any disciple of the Master, or subject of the heavenly King, fail to rejoice when any of his activities – succour, teaching, preaching, arguing or engaging in dialogue – ends in someone else coming to know the Father's love and to respond to the Saviour's mission of mercy and redemption?

The application of this to dialogue is clear enough. But it has been made even more obvious by the comments of a distinguished Hindu writer on religion and philosophical questions, Dr R. Sundarara Rajan of Madras. In a recent comment on current developments in the field of Hindu-Christian dialogue, Newbigin writes:

> He points out that the emphasis upon a self-critical attitude, the demand that each party should try to see things from within the mind of the other, and the disavowal of any attempt by either side to question the faith of the others can easily mean that dialogue is simply an exercise in the mutual confirmation of different beliefs with all the really critical questions excluded. 'If it is impossible to lose one's faith as a result of an encounter with another faith, then I feel that the dialogue has been made safe from all possible risks.'[3] A dialogue which is safe from all possible risks is no true dialogue. The Christian will go into dialogue believing that the sovereign power of the Spirit can use the occasion for the radical conversion of his partner as well as of himself (*The Open Secret*, p.211).

But does this quotation mean that the Christian who enters into dialogue with someone from another faith may himself be converted? To this question there are two answers. First, it is obvious from the fact that Lesslie Newbigin uses the word 'conversion' to refer to the effect, on both Peter and Cornelius, of their encounter, that he does not by any means confine its use to a fundamental change of religion, but extends it to any change of outlook or attitude. This is crystal clear from the words which immediately follow the above quotation, which read: 'When we speak of the Holy Spirit we are speaking of the one who glorifies Christ by taking all the gifts of God and

[3]R. Sundarara Rajan, 'Negations: An Article on Dialogue among Religions', in *Religion and Society* 21, no. 4, p.74.

showing them to the church as the treasury of Christ (John 16:14f.)... The Spirit is not in the possession of the church but is Lord over the church, guiding the church from its limited, partial, and distorted understanding and embodiment of the truth into the fullness of the truth in Jesus who is the one in whom all things consist' (Col. 1:17). And he had already made it abundantly clear that the Christian's 'frame of reference', in dialogue as in all else, must be that 'Jesus Christ is Lord'.

Inevitably, however, there is also another answer. True dialogue cannot be 'made safe from all possible risks'. As Newbigin goes on to say:

> The Christian who enters into dialogue with people of other faiths and ideologies is accepting the risk. But to put *my* Christianity at risk is precisely the way by which I can confess Jesus Christ as Lord – Lord over all worlds and Lord over my faith. It is only as the church accepts the risk that the promise is fulfilled that the Holy Spirit will take all the treasures of Christ, scattered by the Father's bounty over all the peoples and cultures of mankind, and declare them to the church as the possession of Jesus (*The Open Secret*, p.212).

To put much of this in other words, in such dialogue a clear distinction will inevitably have to be made between what we may term 'empirical Christianity' and the gospel. What Christians have made of their faith — or even of the gospel – is wide open to criticism; and we must always be ready to acknowledge this. Indeed, one of the most obvious enrichments for the Christian participant in dialogue is a new apprehension of the difference between the essential gospel and its incarnation in empirical Christianity. But we must equally allow the non-Christian participant to distinguish between the essence of his faith and its empirical manifestations. And this is precisely what we all too often fail to do. As Klostermaier puts it:

> He who has understood the meaning of dialogue will not want to have anything more to do with academic dalliance or a science of comparative religion, behaving

as if it stood above all religions. He will also not want to know anything more of a certain kind of theology that works 'without presuppositions' and pleases itself in manipulating definitions and formulas and forgets about man, who is the main concern. He will be more and more pulled into what is called 'spirituality'; the real life of the mind. I wanted to see a famous man in Benares, a sagacious philosopher, feared by many as a merciless critic of Christian theology. I had my own reasons for paying him a visit. He was polite, invited me for tea and then mounted the attack. I let him talk his fill, without saying a word myself. Then I started to talk about the things I had begun to understand within the dialogue – quite positively Christian. We got into a sincere, good, deep discussion. He had intended to send me away after ten minutes. When I left after two hours, he had tears in his eyes . . .

The real dialogue takes place in an ultimate, personal depth; it does not have to be a talking about religion. But something does distinguish real dialogue: the challenge. Dialogue challenges both partners, takes them out of the security of their own prisons their philosophy and theology have built for them, confronts them with reality, with truth . . . a truth that demands all . . . All of a sudden the shallowness of all religious routine was laid bare, the compromise with the world, that which is essentially un-Christian in so many things that bear Christ's name . . . If dialogue is taken seriously, Christianity must be deeply sincere and upright – different from what it is now (Klostermaier, pp.98f. and 102f.).

These quotations vividly portray the essential difference between true dialogue and either straight evangelism or theological argument. But they also demonstrate that the clear-cut line that some would draw between dialogue and evangelism is itself misleading; for the Christian participant must of necessity speak of Christ and what he means to him — and he may, at any moment, find that the dialogue has undergone a metamorphosis, and that he is pointing his friend to the One who alone can meet man's deepest needs.

Church-building

Much has been written of late about 'cross-cultural' evangelism, and about the mistakes that have been made in the past in a misguided attempt to impose an 'institutional church' of a Western type on converts from a very different background. This whole subject has been discussed in detail by Roland Allen[4], Donald McGavran[5], M. R. Bradshaw[6], Newbigin[7] himself, and in the literature that has resulted from the Lausanne Congress, *inter alia*. One of the chief points of emphasis, and rightly so, has been the difference between what has been termed the 'mission station' approach, on the one hand (with the resultant alienation of the convert, in an unnecessary way, from his family, tribe and culture) and the 'people's movement' approach, on the other – and even the manifest difficulty there is, for example, in making educated converts from Islam fit happily (and bring their Muslim relatives and friends) into a church largely composed of Hindu converts from a very different background. There is much substance in both these related problems, and a number of helpful suggestions have been made. But we must always remember the vital importance that Paul attached to preserving the essential unity of converts from Judaism and paganism, in spite of their radically different traditions, and must strive for a solution which will combine a tolerance for cultural differences with a confession (and demonstration) of the basic unity we all have in Christ Jesus – whatever may be the failings of the 'institutional church'.

If there is one thing about which I become increasingly convinced, it is this: that the living God of the Bible is no pale, remote, philosophical abstraction – whether of the Greek or Indian variety. Far from it. He *loves* his creatures; and this at once makes him 'vulnerable'. Nor did he create the world as some sort of ploy, or even as the spontaneous expression of his creative genius. His *supreme* purpose, as

[4]*Cf. Missionary Methods: St Paul's or Ours?* and *The Ministry of the Spirit* (ed. D. M. Paton).
[5]*Cf.* 'The Dimensions of World Evangelization' (Lausanne Congress paper).
[6]*Cf. Church Growth through Evangelism in Depth.*
[7]*Cf. The Open Secret.*

it seems to me, was 'bringing many sons to glory' (the glory, that is, of being real sons and daughters of God) – an experience that begins here on earth but will be consummated only when we are at last 'conformed to the likeness of his Son, that he might be the firstborn among many brothers' (Rom. 8:29). But this could be achieved only in a world of moral probation, with all the temptation, suffering and even sin (hateful though this is to a holy God) that this would inevitably entail. There was only one remedy that even supreme Love could devise. He came himself, in the person of his Son, not just to visit us, but to share our nature, to bear the full bitterness of temptation, to learn obedience in the school of suffering and to make the supreme sacrifice for our sin. At the cross he, who was himself without sin, 'was made . . . sin for us, so that in him we might become the righteousness of God' (2 Cor. 5:21). To rebels like us, omnipotence may be frightening or may harden us in our rebellion; but love to the uttermost can break even the hardest heart.

So our one purpose – whether in proclamation, argument, dialogue or fellowship – should be that we may be enabled, 'together with all God's people, to grasp how wide and long and high and deep is the love of Christ, and to know this love that surpasses knowledge – that [we] may be filled to the measure of all the fullness of God' (Eph. 3:18f.). Thank God, we can end (again with the apostle): 'Now to him who is able to do immeasurably more than all we ask or imagine, according to his power that is at work within us, to him be glory in the church and in Christ Jesus throughout all generations, for ever and ever! Amen' (Eph. 3:20f.).

Bibliography

(This is not a reading list, but is confined to books and articles quoted or cited in this book. It does not include those authors whose recent books in this field are noted (together with the necessary details) in the Foreword – unless, of course, they are quoted or cited again later.)

Alexander, Brooks, 'The Rise of Cosmic Humanism: What is Religion?', in *S.C.P. Journal* (Spiritual Counterfeits Project), Vol. 5, No. 1 (Berkeley, Winter 1981–2).

Allegro, J. M., *The Sacred Mushroom and the Cross* (London, 1973).

Allen, E. L., *Christianity among the Religions* (London, 1960).

Allen, Roland, *The Ministry of the Spirit* (London, 1960).

—— *Missionary Methods: St Paul's or Ours?* (London, 1968).

Anderson, J. N. D., *Christianity: the Witness of History* (London, 1969).

—— *Christianity and Comparative Religion* (London, 1970).

—— 'Reflections on Law: Natural, Divine and Positive', in *Faith and Thought* (Victoria Institute, London, 1956).

—— 'The Relevance of Oriental and African Legal Studies' (Inaugural Lecture, School of Oriental and African Studies) (London, 1954).

Anderson, Norman, *God's Law and God's Love* (London, 1980).

—— *The Mystery of the Incarnation* (London, 1978).

Atkinson, James, 'Salvation', in *Dictionary of Christian Theology* (ed. Alan Richardson, London, 1969).

Aurobindo, Sri, *Essays on the Gītā* (Madras and New York, 1950).

Barrett, C. K., *A Commentary on the Epistle to the Romans* (London, 1971).

Basham, A. L., *The Wonder that was India* (London, 1954).

—— 'Hinduism' and 'Jainism', in A Concise Encyclopedia of Living Faiths (ed. R. C. Zaehner, London, 1977).

Bevan, Edwyn R., *Hellenism and Christianity* (London, 1921).

—— *The History of Christianity in the Light of Modern Knowledge* (London, 1929).

Binyon, Laurence, *Akbar* (London, 1932).

Blavatsky, H. P., *The Secret Doctrine* (London, 1909).

Bornkamm, Günther, 'The Significance of the Historical Jesus for Faith', in *What can we know about Jesus?* (Essays on the New Quest by Ferdinand Hahn, Wenzel Lohff and Günther Bornkamm) (Edinburgh, 1969).

Bradshaw, M. R., *Church Growth through Evangelism in Depth* (Pasadena, 1969).

Brandon, S. G. F., *Man and his Destiny in the Great Religions* (Manchester, 1962).

Breckinridge, Robert J., *The Knowledge of God* (New York, 1858).

Bruce, F. F., *The Epistle of Paul to the Romans* (London, 1963).

—— *The Epistle to the Hebrews* (London, 1963).

—— 'Melchizedek', in *The Illustrated Bible Dictionary* (Leicester, 1980).

Caird, G. B., *The Gospel of Luke* (London, 1963).

—— 'The Christological Basis of Christian Hope', in *The Christian Hope* (SPCK Theological Collections 13, London, 1970).

Calvin, John, *The Epistles of Paul to the Romans and Thessalonians* (Edinburgh, 1960).

—— *The Epistles to the Hebrews and 1 and 2 Peter* (Edinburgh, 1963).

Conze, Edward, 'Buddhism: The Mahāyāna', in *A Concise Encyclopedia of Living Faiths* (ed. R. C. Zaehner, London, 1977).

Cragg, Kenneth, *The Call of the Minaret* (New York, 1956).

—— *The Christian and Other Religion* (Oxford, 1977).

Davis, Charles, *Christ and the World Religions* (London, 1970).

Deissmann, G. A., *Light from the Ancient East* (London, 1927).

Derrett, J. D. M., *The Anastasis* (Shipston-on-Stour, 1982).

Dewick, E. C., *The Christian Attitude to Other Religions* (Cambridge, 1953).

Dodd, C. H., *The Founder of Christianity* (London, 1971).

Dowsett, Dick, *God, That's Not Fair!* (Sevenoaks, 1983).

Dunne, Carrin, *Conversations between Buddha and Jesus,* quoted by Sebastian Moore in *The Inner Loneliness* (London, 1982).

Eliot, Charles, *Hinduism and Buddhism* (London, 1921).

Ellison, H. L., 'Pharisees', in *The Illustrated Bible Dictionary* (Leicester, 1980).

Erhard, Werner, Article on the 'Self' in *The Graduate Review* (magazine of the *est* organization), Nov. 1976, and in *East West Journal*, Sept. 1974.

Farmer, H. H., *Revelation and Religion* (London, 1954).

Geldenhuys, N., *Commentary on the Gospel of Luke* (London, 1952).

Gelson, A., 'Sadducees', in *The Illustrated Bible Dictionary* (Leicester, 1980).

Hahn, Ferdinand, 'The Quest of the Historical Jesus', in *What can we know about Jesus?* (Essays on the New Quest by Ferdinand Hahn, Wenzel Lohff and Günther Bornkamm) (Edinburgh, 1969).

Hebblethwaite, Brian, 'Incarnation – the Essence of Christianity', in *Theology*, March 1977.

Hendriksen, W., *The Gospel of John* (London, 1961).

Hick, John, *Christianity at the Centre* (London, 1968), enlarged and

republished as *The Centre of Christianity* (London, 1977).
—— *God and the Universe of Faiths* (London, 1973).
—— *God Has Many Names* (London, 1980).
—— 'Christian Theology and Inter-Religious Dialogue', in *World Faiths*, No. 103, Autumn 1977.
—— 'Jesus and the World Religions', in *The Myth of God Incarnate* (ed. John Hick, London, 1977).
Hinnells, John R. (ed.), *Comparative Religion in Education* (Newcastle, 1970).
—— 'Zoroastrianism' and 'Parsees' in *The World's Religions* (A Lion Handbook, Tring, 1982).
Holmes, John Haynes, Preface to D. R. Williams, *World Religions and the Hope for Peace* (Boston, 1951).
Hooft, W. A. Visser 't, *No Other Name* (London, 1963).
Hooke, S. H., 'Christianity and the Mystery Religions', in *Judaism and Christianity* (ed. W. O. E. Oesterley, London, 1937), Vol. 1, *The Age of Transition.*
Horner, I. B., 'Buddhism: The Theravāda', in *A Concise Encyclopedia of Living Faiths* (ed. R. C. Zaehner, London, 1977).
Hughes, T. P., *Dictionary of Islam* (London, 1895).
Hume, R. E., *The World's Living Religions* (London, 1959).
Huxley, A., *The Perennial Philosophy* (London, 1946).
James, E. O., *Christianity and Other Religions* (London, 1968).
—— *In the Fulness of Time* (London, 1935).
Kidner, D., *Genesis* (London, 1967).
Klostermaier, Klaus, *Hindu and Christian in Vrindaban* (London, 1969).
Küng, Hans, *On Being a Christian* (New York, 1976).
—— See also in *Christian Revelation and World Religions* (ed. J. Neuner, London, 1967).
Kuyper, Abraham, *Encyclopedia of Sacred Theology* (New York, 1898).
Laski, Harold, *Reflections on Revolutions in our Times* (London, 1968).
Lawrence, D. H., *Lady Chatterley's Lover* (London, 1928).
—— *The Man Who Died* (London, 1931).
Lewis, C. S., *Miracles* (London, 1947).
Lewis, H. D. and Slater, R. L., *World Religions* (London, 1966).
Lightfoot, J. B., *Saint Paul's Epistle to the Galatians* (London, 1900).
Lightfoot, R. H., *St John's Gospel. A Commentary* (ed. C. F. Evans, Oxford, 1956).
Lyall, Leslie, *Red Sky at Night* (London, 1969).
Macdonald, D. B., *Muslim Theology, Jurisprudence and Constitutional Theory* (New York, 1903).
McGavran, Donald, 'The Dimensions of World Evangelization' (Lausanne Congress paper).
Marshall, I. H., *The Epistles of John* (Grand Rapids, 1978).
Mason, Philip, *The Dove in Harness* (London, 1976).
Masters, R. E. L. and Houston, Jean, *The Varieties of Psychedelic Experience* (New York, 1966).
Mbiti, John S., *Concepts of God in Africa* (London, 1970).
Metz, Wulf, 'One Goal, Many Paths', in *The World's Religions* (A Lion

Handbook, Tring, 1982).

Metzger, B. M., 'Mystery Religions and Early Christianity', in his *Historical and Literary Studies* (Leiden, 1968).

Montefiore, Hugh, 'The Church and the Jews' (Lecture, Birmingham, 1983).

Moore, Sebastian, *The Inner Loneliness* (London, 1982).

Morgan, G. Campbell, *The Acts of the Apostles* (London, 1924).

—— *The Crises of the Christ* (London, 1945).

Motyer, J. A., 'Idolatry', in *The Illustrated Bible Dictionary* (Leicester, 1980).

Moule, C. F. D., *The Origin of Christology* (Cambridge, 1977).

—— See also article on the pre-existence of Jesus in *Theologica Evangelica*, Vol. III, No. 3, Sept. 1975.

Neill, Stephen C., *Christian Faith and Other Faiths* (Oxford, 1961).

Neuner, Joseph (ed.), *Christian Revelation and World Religions* (London, 1967).

Newbigin, Lesslie, *A Faith for this one World* (London, 1961).

—— *The Finality of Christ* (London, 1969).

—— *The Open Secret* (Grand Rapids, 1978).

Newing, Edward G., 'Religions of Pre-Literary Societies', in *The World's Religions* (ed. Norman Anderson, London, 1975).

Oesterley, W. O. E. (ed.), *Judaism and Christianity* (London, 1937).

Pahnke, W. N., 'L.S.D. and Religious Experience', in *L.S.D., Man, Drugs and Society* (ed. R. C. DeBold and R. C. Leaf, London, 1969).

Panikkar, R., *The Unknown Christ of Hinduism* (London, 1965).

Pannenberg, Wolfhart, *Jesus: God and Man* (London, 1968).

Parkes, James, *Conflict of the Church and Synogogue* (London, 1969).

Parrinder, E. G., *An Introduction to Asian Religions* (London, 1957).

Percy, J. O. (ed.), *Facing the Unfinished Task* (Grand Rapids, 1961).

Polanyi, Michael, *Personal Knowledge* (London, 1958).

Radhakrishnan, Sarvepalli, *Recovery of Faith* (London, 1956), quoted by Stephen Neill in *Christian Faith and Other Faiths* (Oxford, 1961).

Rahner, Karl, *Theological Investigations*, Vol. 14 (London, 1976).

Ramsey, Michael, *Sacred and Secular* (London, 1965).

Robinson, J. A. T., *Twelve New Testament Studies* (London, 1962).

—— 'Resurrection in the New Testament', in *The Interpreter's Dictionary of the Bible*, Vol. 4 (New York, 1962).

Roseveare, Helen, *Living Faith* (London, 1980).

Schaeffer, F. A., *Escape from Reason* (London, 1968).

Schmidt, W., *The Origin and Growth of Religion* (trans. H. J. Rose, London, 1931).

Schonfield, Hugh, *The Passover Plot* (London, 1965).

Schweitzer, Albert, *Paul and His Interpreters* (London, 1912).

Sharpe, Eric J., 'The Comparative Study of Religion in Historical Perspective', in *Comparative Religion in Education* (ed. J. R. Hinnells, Newcastle, 1970).

Shillito, Edward, *Jesus of the Scars and Other Poems* (London, 1919).

Smart, Ninian, *World Religions: A Dialogue* (London, 1960; Pelican Books, 1966).

Smith, Wilfred Cantwell, *The Faith of Other Men* (New York and London, 1965).

—— *The Meaning and End of Religion* (New York, 1964).

Spinoza, Benedict de, *Ethics* (London, 1910).

Stace, W. T., *Mysticism and Philosophy* (London, 1961).

—— *Time and Eternity* (Oxford, 1952).

Tasker, R. V. G., *The General Epistle of James* (London, 1956).

Temple, William, *Readings in St John's Gospel* (London, 1943).

Tillich, Paul, *Christianity and the Encounter of the World Religions* (New York, 1964).

Tinsley, E. J., 'Mysticism', in *Dictionary of Christian Theology* (ed. Alan Richardson, London, 1969).

Toynbee, Arnold, *Christianity among the Religions of the World* (London, 1958).

Trickett, Rachel, 'Imagination and Belief', in *God Incarnate: Story and Belief* (ed. A. E. Harvey, London, 1981).

Vivekānanda, Swami, *Inspired Talks* (New York, 1958).

Warfield, B. B., 'Are They Few That Be Saved?', in *Biblical and Theological Studies* (Philadelphia, 1952).

—— 'The Development of the Doctrine of Infant Salvation', in *Studies in Theology* (New York, 1932).

—— 'Jesus Christ the Propitiation for the Whole World', in *Selected Shorter Writings of Benjamin B. Warfield I* (New Jersey, 1976).

Zaehner, R. C. (ed.), *A Concise Encyclopedia of Living Faiths* (London, 1977).

—— *Hinduism* (Oxford, 1966).

—— *Mysticism, Sacred and Profane* (Oxford, 1957).

Zwemer, S. M., *The Influence of Animism on Islam* (New York, 1920).

Index of biblical references

Index of authors

General index

Lesser Vehicle *See* Hīnayāna, Theravāda Buddhism
Liberation *See moksha*
Lie (the) 61
Life Spring 126
Light 34, 131, 133, 161, 164f.
Living God 125, 135, 193f.
Logos *See* Word
Love of God 93, 113, 123, 128 – 131, 178, 194
Lovers of Jesus 157
LSD 41

Magic 60, 103, 115f.
Mahāvīra 33, 61
Mahāyāna Buddhism 63, 88, 91, **94 – 98, 102 – 103**, 121
Mahdī 67
Mahomed *See* Muhammad
mantras 103
Martyrdom 97
māyā (illusion) 59, 89f., 101, 119
Mediator 42, 63, 146
Meditation 39, 62, 88, 91f.
Mercy of God 43, 106, 125, 148, 151, 153 – 155, 160, 168, 175
Messiah, Messianic 29, 67 – 70, 72f., 82, 141, 157f., 160f., 178f.
Metempsychosis 65
Middle Way 102f.
Miracles 150
Missionary urgency 155
Mohammed *See* Muhammad
moksha (liberation, release) 89f., 119
Monasticism 88
Monism, monistic 43, 59, 92, 118f., 122, 126f., 130f.
Monotheism, monotheist, monotheistic 64, 68, 70, 72,

Monotheism (*cont.*) 105, 115 – 117, 119, 128, 135, 180f.
Moral conduct, responsibility 15, 129f.
Moral Rearmament 19
Mosaic law 68, 87, 146, 152, 157, 183
Moses 31, 113, 141, 143, 157
Muhammad 18, 33, 64f., 137n., 187
mujaddid See Reformer
mujtahids 66
mukhālafa 124
Mushrooms 39
Muslim(s) 13, 38f., 41, 56f., 64 – 68, 97f., 124, 146, 160, 163, 173, 181, 187
Musta'līs 66
Mu'tazila 181
Mysteries, mystery religions **51 – 56**, 104f., 180
Mysticism, mystics 16, 22, 34, **37 – 45**, 92
Myth, mythology 56, 64, 86, 104, 115, 127, 137, 180

Nationalism 84
'Native American Church' 39, 41n.
Nature 150
Nature god 56
Nature mysticism 41, 43
Nature religions 55, 60
Neo-platonism 38, 124f.
New Covenant *See* Covenant
New Testament 15, 35, 45f., 48, 52f., 55, 57, 70, 72, 76 – 78, 85, 98f., 104, 112, 124f., 129, 131f., 139, 147f., 156, 180, 188
Nirvāna 63, 87f., 91f., 94 – 96, 102
Nizārīs 66
Non-Christian religions **169 – 174**